Recognizing the Intrinsic

PROPERTY OF:
COMPASSION IN WORLD FARMING
INFORMATION LIBRARY
PETERSFIELD GU32 3EH
PLEASE BOOK OUT BEFORE BORROWING

ANIMALS IN PHILOSOPHY AND SCIENCE

Editorial Board of Animals in Philosophy and Science

M. Bekoff, University of Colorado, Boulder, CO, USA
R. Burkhardt, University of Illinois, Urbana, IL, USA
P. Cohn, The Pennsylvania State University, Uniontown, PE, USA
Tj. de Cock Buning, University of Leiden, Leiden, the Netherlands
J. Fentress, Dalhousie University, Halifax, Nova Scotia, Canada
J. Koolhaas, University of Groningen, Groningen, the Netherlands
D. Macer, University of Tsukuba, Tsukuba Science City, Ibaraki, Japan
W. Van der Steen, Free University, Amsterdam, the Netherlands
D. Broom, University of Cambridge, Cambridge, U.K.

Editorial Board (continued): series editors

M. Dol, University of Leiden, Leiden, the Netherlands
S. Kasanmoentalib, Free University, Amsterdam, the Netherlands
S. Lijmbach, Wageningen Agricultural University, Wageningen, the Netherlands
E. Rivas, University of Nijmegen, Nijmegen, the Netherlands
R. van den Bos, University of Leiden, Leiden, the Netherlands

The **APS** series functions as an interdisciplinary platform for discussion between different disciplines in philosophy and science on topics concerning animals. Issues will include: animal consciousness, evolutionary psychology, animals in society, cultural images of animal ethics.

Animals have become a respectable subject in philosophy, science and politics, especially since the 1970s. After two decades of research it is time to bring together the results from these different disciplines. The series **Animals in Philosophy and Science** will offer a platform for discussion of these research results and for interdisciplinary research into animal consciousness, evolutionary psychology, animals in society, animal ethics and related subjects. This forum will stimulate discussion on animals in society at large and encourage positive change in our treatment of and perspective on nonhuman animals. Disciplines involved range from philosophy, psychology, ethology and biology, to neuropsychology, anthropology and other sciences. The series is directed at researchers in the relevant disciplines, advisors on public policies, administrators, animal ethicists, and the general public interested in the academic analysis of animal issues. Publications will vary from volumes of discussion on one specific subject and proceedings of conferences, to dissertations and books by one or more authors on research relevant to the series' manifesto. Suggestions or manuscripts for books can be submitted to the editorial board for their consideration.

Recognizing the Intrinsic Value of Animals

Beyond Animal Welfare

Eds.
Marcel Dol
Martje Fentener van Vlissingen
Soemini Kasanmoentalib
Thijs Visser
Hub Zwart

1999

Van Gorcum

© 1999, Van Gorcum & Comp. B.V., P.O. Box 43, 9400 AA Assen, The Netherlands

All rights reserved. No part of this publication may be reproduced, stored in a retrieval system, or transmitted, in any form or by any means, electronic, mechanical, photocopying, recording, or otherwise, without the prior permission of the Publisher.

NUGI 611

ISBN 90 232 3469 3

Print: Van Gorcum, Assen, The Netherlands

Contents

Introduction

Part I
Intrinsic value of animals in public policy development in the Netherlands

1 The use of 'intrinsic value of animals' in the Netherlands
   Frans W.A. Brom 15

2 Intrinsic value and the struggle against anthropocentrism
   Edward van der Tuuk 29

Part II
Intrinsic value of animals: ethical issues

3 Inherent worth and respect for animal integrity
   Bart Rutgers & Robert Heeger 41

4 Intrinsic value and species-specific behaviour
   Ruud van den Bos 53

5 Incompatibility of intrinsic value with genetic manipulation
   Thijs Visser 71

6 Bio-ethics and the intrinsic value of animals
   Henk Verhoog 81

Part III
Intrinsic value: the philosophical issues

7 Intrinsic Value or Intrinsic Valuing?
   Albert W. Musschenga 97

Part IV
The application of the concept of intrinsic value: the case of animal research

8 Intrinsic value of animals used for research
   J. Martje Fentener van Vlissingen 123

9 The real role of 'intrinsic value' in ethical review committees
   Tjard de Cock Buning 133

Introduction

Moral concern for animals is commonly formulated in terms of concern for their welfare. Yet, besides the welfare issue, although highly relevant in itself, the importance of the intrinsic value of animals, defying instrumentalization of the animals involved, has to be recognized as well. The phrase intrinsic value, however, is borrowed from human ethics and has for a considerable period of time been exclusively applied to˙man. If the term is applied to animals, its meaning and import have to be reconsidered. Does it apply to individual animals, for example, or rather to species? Does it apply to domesticated animals in the same manner as it does to their wild relatives? What are the philosophical implications of the recognition of intrinsic value, and what are the practical consequences for our daily interaction with them? This volume contains a philosophical review of the ethical evaluation of animals in terms of intrinsic value, as well as a series of efforts to apply this concept to relevant fields of interest (e.g. domestic animals, biotechnology, wild life, research on animals, intensive breeding). Different point of views are represented and different dilemmas are explored.

In *Part I*, the role of the concept of 'intrinsic value' of animals in public policy development in the Netherlands is reviewed. Frans W.A. Brom draws attention to the way this concept was introduced in the legislation process regarding animal practices. Edward van der Tuuk reflects on the concept of intrinsic value by highlighting some of the recent developments in the field of biotechnology.

In *Part II*, the ethical issues involved in the concept of intrinsic value are addressed. In the contribution of Bart Rutgers and Robert Heeger, two questions are asked. The first question concerns the clause that animals have "a value of their own". How should this clause be interpreted? The authors try to find an interpretation that will offer a criterion. The second question addressed concerns the concept of inherent worth. If one subscribes to the view that animals have inherent worth, one assumes a basic attitude of moral respect for them. Yet how should this attitude of respect be characterized? The authors propose to describe it as respect for animal integrity, and put this description in concrete terms by considering some problematical cases from veterinary medicine and animal breeding.

Subsequently, Ruud van den Bos discusses the concept of intrinsic value in relation to the concept of species-specific behaviour. It is argued that it is a (naturalistic) fallacy to attempt to define intrinsic value as a property of an individual animal based upon certain objective characteristics. Instead, intrinsic value must be defined as a property of a relationship in terms of meaning or interest.

Thijs Visser discusses the question whether genetic manipulation is compatible with intrinsic value of nature. Usually, two arguments in favor of genetic manipulation are used. Genetic engineering is either regarded as a natural process, occurring in nature as well, or a kind of technique that is basically similar to other techniques developed by mankind in the course of history. Both kinds of arguments are analyze critically and, eventually, rejected. Finally, a short overview is presented of the Dutch policy regarding genetic engineering.

The contribution by Henk Verhoog reflects on some basic problems in the other contributions to Part II. In one way or another, Verhoog points out, the authors involved struggle with the relationship between (factual) knowledge about living organisms, and the morality of our relations to these organisms. The central concepts of these chapters (naturality, species-specific behaviour, autonomy and integrity) are all used with both moral and biological connotations, with the concept of the intrinsic value of animals as a unifying category. It can have this unifying function because of its key meaning: "having a value of its own", by itself, independent of its usefulness (its instrumental value) for human beings.

In *Part III*, the philosophical aspects of the concept of intrinsic value are addressed in an extensive contribution by Albert W. Musschenga. As every other species, Musschenga tells us, humans have to extract from their natural environment the resources they need for their living. In contradistinction to other species, however, they lack the adaptation to a specific ecological niche. Therefore, they have to change their environment to make it hospitable for them. In this process of interaction with his natural environment man creates culture. There is a growing insight, however, that man has to regulate his interactions with his natural environment in order to prevent the destruction of the living conditions for himself, or at least for future human generations. Enlightened self-interest should motivate him to become more conscious of the indirect and long-term effects of his interactions with nature. But for many humans self-interest is not the only reason to worry about the fate of their fellow natural entities. For them it is not enough that humans start to care about natural entities because and insofar as the well-being of existing or future human generations is at stake. In their view the value of natural entities is not exhausted by their usefulness to human needs and goals and human interactions with their natural environment should be regulated, that is: contained by moral principles. For many, the notion of the intrinsic value of nature is the cornerstone of a non-anthropocentric conception of environmental ethics. Many environmentalists also take for granted that intrinsic value is *objective*. Not all environmental ethicists are convinced that an environmental ethic needs to be non-anthropocentric. They prefer an ethic founded on an enlightened anthropocentrism, either because they reject non-anthropocentrism on normative grounds or because they have doubts about the motivational force of a non-anthropocentric ethic. Those who assert that nature has intrinsic value consider the range of such an ethic to be too limited. They find that an environmental ethic should be able to provide reasons for protecting even those natural entities that will probably never be of any interest for humans. In his conribution, Musschenga takes sides with the latter position and grants that the idea of nature having intrinsic value is indispensable for a non-anthropocentric environmental ethic.

Finally, in *Part IV*, the concept of intrinsic value is applied to one animal practice in particular, namely research on animals. Martje Fentener van Vlissingen, in her general overview, points to some of the problems that arise whenever the concept is actually applied by questioning the significance of certain characteristics of animals, such as complexity and naturalness (authenticity). Does the intrinsic value of animals allow for quantification? Is intrinsic value affected by human intervention? And what is the relationship of intrinsic value with welfare, integrity and dignity?

Tjard the Cock Buning analyzes the role the concept of intrinsic value really plays in the review procedures of animal ethics committees. He checked the minutes of the ethical review committees of which of he was a member for the past five years and asked himself how often the concept was actually discussed. He concludes that intrinsic value is an adequate moral concept to express moral concern regarding issues like "painlessly killing animals" ("euthanasia"), xenotransplantation and cloning. It is a key concept to express moral concerns regarding new technologies that distinguishes in a sophisticated manner moral arguments from anxieties, hesitations and feelings of uneasiness.

Acknowledgments

The editors are grateful for the support received from the following persons and organizations: The Dutch Ministry of Agriculture, Nature Management and Fisheries (LNV), Solvay Duphar B.V., The Netherlands School for Research in Practical Philosophy, Priscilla Cohn, Darryl Macer, Susanne Lijmbach (Series editor), Peter Rijnhart (layout).

The Editors

Part I

Intrinsic Value of Animals in Public Policy Development in the Netherlands

1

The use of 'intrinsic value of animals' in the Netherlands[1]

Frans W.A. Brom

1. Introduction

The *Preamble* of the *Flora and Fauna Bill*, debated in the Netherlands in 1997, states that "it is desirable to bring together the disparate statutory rules concerning the protection of wild species of flora and fauna in a single Act, particularly with a view to improved harmonization of the rules, in the interest of the protection of those wild species of flora and fauna and, where it applies to species of fauna, also of the recognition of the intrinsic value of the animals concerned". Why is respect for the intrinsic value of animals of essential importance? The Minister of Agriculture explains that "insofar as human intervention in relation to protected animals is permitted, it should be carried out with respect for the animals. That is the background to this part of the preamble".

During the parliamentary debate on this Bill[2] various members of parliament took the view that to lay down such a principle in the preamble only is insufficient. It should be incorporated in the body of the Act itself. This would provide a much firmer basis for those who are to apply the law. In this manner, moreover, the principle could be "tested directly". The question was, however, what the behavioural and legal consequences of incorporating this principle in the Act itself would be. For instance, would it imply that hunting animals is no longer regarded as permitted? That it is rather difficult to clarify exactly what the incorporation of the principle would entail in terms of the implementation of the Act, becomes apparent if one looks at one of the arguments used by the principal advocate of statutory embodiment. "On the basis of this general principle", he stated in parliament, "one could conclude that a list of animals that may be hunted is not permissible, but one could equally conclude that such a list is in fact permissible". In the parliamentary debate there was consensus as to the importance of the recognition of the intrinsic value of animals as a common point of departure. At the same time, however, there was no consensus in terms of the concrete behavioural and legal consequences of this recognition. In the words used in the parliamentary debate: "Intrinsic value is not at issue: what we are concerned here with is its interpretation, which is different for everyone".

This debate on the *Flora and Fauna Bill* is typical of parliamentary debates on animal protection legislation in The Netherlands. There is consensus regarding the recognition of the "intrinsic value of animals" as common point of departure, but no consensus as to the behavioural and legal consequences of such a recognition. The concept of intrinsic value of animals functioned as a key concept in the sociopolitical debate and the legislative process ever since 1981. In spite of the broad acceptance of the term, however, the main goal of those who introducing it - to improve the lives of animals in intensive husbandry systems - has not been reached. Does this imply that the recognition of intrinsic value is practical without consequences?

This is the question that provoked this contribution. While relying on a reconstruction of the role the concept actually played in sociopolitical debate,[3] I will maintain that this concept (however vague) fulfills an important, persuasive function and constitutes a common point of departure for animal protection. Improvements of the living conditions of animals in animal husbandry, however, depend neither on further clarification of the concept, nor on further codification and legislature. Rather, concrete improvements will depend on the reconstruction of animal husbandry itself. It is now time to develop housing-systems that will allow for sustainable animal husbandry that involve acceptable levels of animal welfare.

2. Animal protection legislation before 1981

To begin with, I will consider the (first) Dutch penal code (1886) in which animals were protected against cruelty. In 1920 the code was changed into a code for the protection of animals against maltreatment. The latter concept ("maltreatment") remained the key concept until 1981, while its meaning was clarified by the Animal Experimentation Act of 1977.

2.1 The protection of animals against cruelty

At first, animal protection legislation concentrated on the question of cruelty by humans towards animals. Since 1886 cruelty towards animals is forbidden under the Dutch Penal Code. According to art. 254 (and later also 455) maltreatment of animals is liable to punishment. This legislation is based on a mixed set of reasons. Firstly, it involves the so-called "classical" reason for preventing cruelty towards animals. Animals need to be protected against maltreatment, not because of the animals themselves, but because of the consequences maltreatment has for interhuman morality. Indifference towards animal suffering, or (even worse) taking pleasure in it, degrades the moral quality of the person involved and may extinguish important aspects of moral sensibility. This classical argument against cruelty towards animals, however, is mixed with another reason: cruelty towards animals is wrong because animals can suffer, and suffering is bad.

In his defense of the first Penal Code, minister Modderman appealed to this argument when he stated: "An animal, as long as it lives, is not in all respects identical with a thing. Someone who tears his book into pieces, will be considered a fool at worst; someone who does the same with a living dog or cat would learn, even from the simplest workman - whose instinctive sense of justice is in many respects of more value than the reflections of a great number of scholars - that he has done *injustice*." (Schmidt 1891, 370). Although his conclusion that legislation against cruelty to animals was necessary, was agreed to by the majority of Parliament

Members, his line of argument was not, as a number of members supported art. 254 on the "classical" grounds.

This Penal Code of 1886, however, was not very effective. One of the problems involved the question whether cruelty implies cruel intentions. In october 1887 the Dutch Supreme Court ruled that under this article the presence of "cruel intentions" had to be explicitly proven - and the "classical" argument against cruelty towards animals was behind this ruling. But as the presence of cruel intentions was difficult, if not impossible to prove, the law seized to function.

2.2. The protection of animals against maltreatment

In 1920, the Penal Code was changed. The idea that cruelty towards animals was problematic because of the cruel intentions was now abandoned. The new law concentrated on maltreatment. The idea of proportionality became the central issue. Causing pain or injury (actively or by neglect) without reasonable purpose, or by exceeding the limits of the acceptable, was now liable to punishment. Cruelty towards animals no longer referred to cruel intentions but to unreasonable purpose. This change of the law, however, was not very effective either. Again, the Supreme Court gave a minimalist interpretation of the law. According to its ruling, nearly every purpose could render an act reasonable. Aesthetic reasons, for instance, were seen as reasonable (such as docking a dog). As a consequence of this, very few cases were brought into court, resulting in even fewer convictions. Animal Protection Societies were unhappy with this legal practice. Before the Second World War they took several initiatives in order to have a general Animal Act established, but none succeeded.

During the Second World War, animal protectionists co-operated with the Nazi occupiers to produce a new bill. Its approval, however, was delayed, because it was not *kriegswichtig* (important for warfare) enough. After the World War, the Dutch Society for the Protection of Animals produced several draft bills. Some of these were debated in parliament, but it did not come to actual parliamentary reading. In 1955 a draft *Animal Protection Act*, prepared by a governmental committee, was brought into parliament. This bill was debated in parliament for 6 years. In the course of this debate, the act was toned down. In 1961 it became operative. This Act was meant to make art. 254 and 455 of the Penal Code better applicable. From the 1960's onwards, animal husbandry became more and more intensive. This was supported by agricultural policy and the quest for sufficient, safe and cheap food. Despite of the economical and food-policy successes of these new husbandry systems, there were strong and active protests against it. It was said that animals in these housing systems suffered; not only because of direct injuries, but also because of the confinement that made it impossible for them to behave in certain species-specific ways. Often, they were not able to lie down, to turn around or to stand up. This transformed them into "Animal Machines" (Harrison 1964). In several countries public protests incited inquiries into the welfare of animals kept under intensive husbandry systems, for example the Brambell-report in the UK in 1965. In the Netherlands a committee was established in 1973. In 1975 it issued a report that pointed at animal welfare problems in several housing systems and suggested that government action ought to be taken. The 1961 act was not appropriate to exhort the necessary improvements. Therefore, the minister of Agriculture promised in 1974 a new animal welfare legislation. This legislation should improve the welfare situation of animals in the new intensive husbandry practices.

Apart from animal protection legislation, practices involving animals are covered by several other laws as well. Of special interest for our subject is the legislation on the quality of the food and the health of the animals. Since 1920 there existed a so-called "Livestock Act". This act covered, among other things, the way the government would control epidemics of epizootic diseases, like classical pigs fever. Since the 1920's many changes occurred within Veterinary Medicine. Techniques for controlling epizootic diseases improved and the Livestock Act was amended several times. Due to these amendments, it became a rather patchy collection of acts and regulations. Therefore, in 1980 a new bill was brought into parliament: the Animal Health Act. The animal welfare legislation, promised in 1974, was supposed to be covered by this act, but in fact it only restated the maltreatment article. This did not satisfy parliament.

2.3 The protection of animals used in experiments

The Dutch discussion on the protection of laboratory animals used in animal experimentation in The Netherlands is of long standing. Already in 1888 a juridical thesis (Witsen 1888) was written on the subject. In this thesis a license system for animal experimentation was proposed. There were State Committees in 1907 and 1933, that both advised in favour of a licensing system. Only those institutions should be allowed to perform animal experiments that could guarantee "reasonableness". The scientific community protested vigorously against legislation. Scientists are not cruel, they said, and the experiments carried out by them are scientifically sound, and this makes these experiments reasonable by definition. During the Second World War, the legislative process stopped.

During the 1950's, however, the process was resumed. Animal experiments were covered in the 1955 draft of the Animal Protection Act mentioned earlier. However, during parliamentary debate it was removed from the act. When the Act finally became operative in 1961 the animal experiment issue was separated from the general legislation; it became a subject for special legislation.

A special governmental committee was installed to prepare an Experiments on Animals Act. This committee concluded that it is not realistic to outlaw animal experiments, but that there were good reasons for regulating them. The most important reason was the need to protect the animals involved. In 1970 a Proposal was send to parliament. The preamble of the Act stated that protection of animals was the principal argument for regulation. Parliamentary debate amounted in 1977 in the Experiments on Animals Act (EAA). Central in the EAA are three points.

- An animal experiment may only be performed by persons or institutions that have a license. To obtain a license, certain qualifications have to be met. This condition was meant to exempt only those persons who could be expected to perform "reasonable" experiments only.
- Experiments are only allowed for specified goals. These goals should be (a) directly or indirectly in the interest of human or animal health (for instance by improving the quality of food products), or (b) to find an answer to a scientific question. This condition specified the goals that were to be considered as reasonable.

- An experiment is not allowed if, according to an accepted view among experts, an alternative is available. This condition refers to the idea of proportionality. If there is an alternative, an experiment exceeds the limits acceptable for this (reasonable) purpose.

2.4 Conclusion

Before 1981 animal protection legislation is based upon different motives. From 1920 the legislative process concentrates upon the idea of proportionality. According to this idea, it is legitimate to cause pain or injury if, and only if, the purpose is reasonable, and - in the light of the pain or injury - of enough importance. Explication of this idea of proportionality in the Experiments on Animals Act shows that proportionality also implies the absence of a (less problematic) alternative.

By making the reasonableness of the purpose the central concept in animal protection legislation, the law tends to concentrate on specific human acts. Only (direct) pain or (direct) injury caused in a way that does not fit within a reasonable practice can be considered as maltreatment. The confinement of animals within agricultural practice as such, is seen as reasonable because it is embedded in and legitimated by economical rationality: it is considered to be necessary for the production of sufficient, safe and cheap food.

3. Animal protection legislation since 1981

The Netherlands government issued in 1981 the memorandum *Rijksoverheid en Dierenbescherming* (National Government and Animal Protection). In this memorandum, the Dutch government endorsed the "intrinsic value" of the individual animal as an explicit point of departure for its policy on the human-animal relationship. This memorandum had legislative consequences. The *Animal Health and Welfare Act* (AHWA), with its characteristic "no-unless"-structure, is based upon this memorandum and played a crucial role in the revision of the *Experiments on Animals Act*. Thirdly, it played a role in the development of a license-system for animal biotechnology.

3.1 The AHWA and its "no-unless"-structure

In 1985, important things happened within the animal protection legislation. Firstly, the minister of Agriculture issued a new draft for the *Animal Health Act*. This new draft contained an additional chapter on animal welfare regulations. Therefore, the name of the act was changed into *Animal Health and Welfare Act* (AHWA). In the new draft, possibilities were created for Animal Welfare regulations, but hardly any concrete measures were taken. Secondly, the *Dutch Society for the Protection of Animals* again took the initiative for an *Animal Welfare Act* (Boon 1985). Characteristic of this initiative-bill was what came to be known as the "no-unless"-structure. Practices that are detrimental to animal welfare are forbidden *unless* permitted by special regulation. According to this initiative, welfare-regulations *have* to be made. The law forbids injuring animal welfare without regulation. The initiative *Welfare Act* of the *Dutch Society for the Protection of Animals* influenced the parliamentary debate considerably. Parliament wanted the minister of Agriculture to change the welfare chapter of his AHWA in accordance with its "no-unless"-structure. In 1989 a proposal based on this structure was sent to parliament. Parliament however was not satisfied with the changes made and had little confidence in the proposed regulations. As a result, the Minister promised in 1990 to discuss these regulations with parliament before they would become effective. In 1992 parliament passed the revised version of the act. The *Animal Health and Welfare Act* (AHWA) now functions as a general legal framework, basically following the logic of "no, unless". There is, for instance, a special regulation for surgery without veterinary necessity on animals in certain cases. Only those surgical practices that are explicitly mentioned in this regulation, such as removing horns from cattle, are allowed.

The law gave rise to a considerable amount of regulation. The "no, unless"-structure implied that every act or situation that *could* be detrimental to animal welfare had to be regulated. In fact the law obliged the government to prescribe farmers in detail how to handle and house animals. Despite the number of specific regulations, this brought little improvement to the welfare of animals. The legislation has - as the lawyer Willem Bruil, specialised in agriculture, correctly states it (1997, 88) - merely outlawed some excesses. Animal welfare has been contained on its current (low) level. The economic interests of farmers seem to have prevented the effectiveness of the legislative system.

3.2 Modernization of the Animal Experimentation legislation
In 1985 (the year of the changes in the AHWA and the initiative for an *Animal Welfare Act* of the *Dutch Society for the Protection of Animals*), the *Advisory Board on Animal Experiments* wrote an advice on behalf of the Minister of Public Health. In this advice the Advisory Board proposed to institutionalize the discussion on the acceptability of experiments in animal ethics committees. The question whether a certain experiment was acceptable had to be taken out of the hands of those directly involved.

Most research institutions installed *Animal Experiment Committees* (AEC) voluntarily. The idea behind the (voluntary erected) AEC's was self-regulation. The idea was that moral values have to become internalized by those who are the actual moral actors, the researchers in this case (De Cock Buning 1996, 63).

In 1996 the *Animal Experimentation Act* was changed. The Animal Experiment Committees became obligatory. Animal experiments are now allowed only if an Animal Experiment Committee has assessed and approved them. The law also provides guidelines for the membership of these committees. The chair has to be independent and some members should be recruited from outside the institution. Members must also have had some experience with the ethical assessment of experiments. Stricter language is used in the new law when it comes to describing the relation between goal and animal discomfort, and the importance of alternatives is stressed as well. Not only alternatives as such are mentioned, but mention is even made of the famous three "R's" (Russel and Burch 1959): replacement of animals, the refinement of the experiment and the reduction of the number of animals.

During the parliamentary debate, the parliament included an explicit addition in

the act. It had to be in line with the political and moral discussions on which the AHWA was based. Therefore the "intrinsic value" of the animal should have a place in the act. As it was absent in the preamble, the parliament included an addition in the text of the Act itself. Section 1a now reads:
"Any right accorded by or pursuant to this Act shall be exercised in recognition of the intrinsic value of animal life".

3.3 The protection of animal integrity
The "intrinsic value of animals" became an even more central concept in the discussions on the ethical acceptability of animal biotechnology (Brom and Schroten 1993, 1998). In order to answer questions regarding the ethics of animal biotechnology, the Minister of Agriculture installed in 1989 an independent advisory committee. In its report of 1990 the committee takes the intrinsic value of animals as its point of departure. In the report this concept is explained as follows: "Especially the criticism of the use of animals as experimental animals and of livestock housing has resulted in the recognition that animals have a value of their own, or an intrinsic value, besides their instrumental value to man. In other words, man has to respect the intrinsic value of animals. Animals come to fall under the province of ethics, not in the sense that animals are thought to act morally, but in the sense that they are deserving our moral care" (Advisory Committee 1990, p. 8).
The Committee recommends a "no-unless"-policy concerning animal biotechnology. In this respect the Committee Report supports the line of policy of the Dutch government in which, as was indicated above, a "no unless policy" is chosen. In the Report there is no definition of this policy, but it is stated that it implies an ethical "evaluation framework" and criteria through which concrete biotechnological actions concerning animals can be assessed. In this evaluation framework three "phases" are distinguished:
- the acquisition of morally relevant facts with regard to a certain project
- the assessment of the consequences of the project in view of specified values (nature, animals, human health and welfare, environment)
- the weighing of the pros and cons, in the light of the information that becomes available during the preceding phases

This report was followed in the AHWA. A special provision was made for animal biotechnology. The "no unless"-policy from the Welfare chapter was amended for the use of biotechnological techniques on animals. Under the AHWA genetic modification of animals, cloning and the making of chimeras is not permitted *unless* the Minister of Agriculture issues a license. Since this Act is operative (April 1997), the ethical acceptability of every project in the field of animal biotechnology has to be assessed by a committee. Members of the committee are not only experts in different technical fields of biotechnology, (veterinary) medicine and animal husbandry, but also experts in ethology, animal experiments and ethics. These members are not representing certain societal groups like the animal protection movement, consumer groups, industry or science, but they give their independent expert-based opinion on the matter. This committee advises the minister of Agriculture who will take the final decision.
With regard to this decision, two criteria are stipulated in the Act: In article 66 it

is stated that an assent may be given if (1) there are no unacceptable consequences for the health and welfare of the animals and if (2) there are no ethical objections. According to the explanatory memorandum these two criteria are both expressions of the "intrinsic value" of the animals concerned.

Before April 1997, when this system became formally operative, experiments performed under direct jurisdiction of the Minister of Agriculture had to be assessed in accordance with this regulatory framework. At that time, the Leiden based company Gene-Pharming was performing an experiment with a genetically modified bull (named Herman). This experiment was carried out in cooperation with one of the agricultural research institutes under jurisdiction of the minister of agriculture. In this experiment the genetic make up of cattle is changed in order to produce certain proteins in their milk. An ethical review committee of the Ministry of Agriculture assessed this experiment and allowed it (Schroten 1998). Because of uncertainty about the welfare-consequences of the experiment, however, a welfare assessment was made obligatory. This assessment was carried out (Van Reenen and Blokhuis 1993).

In the moral and political discussions following the experiment the discussion focused on the second criterion. What is meant by "ethical objections", what is the relation between these objections and the "intrinsic value" of the animals involved? The crucial concept in this discussion became animal "integrity". Central in this concept is the idea that our moral obligations towards animals, based upon the recognition of their "intrinsic value", go beyond the protection of their welfare (Brom 1997b). A more precise analysis of this concept is elaborated elsewhere in this volume (Rutgers and Heeger).

3.4 Conclusion

Since 1981 the prevention of certain human acts (cruelty, maltreatment) is no longer the sole purpose of the animal protection legislation. The purpose of protecting animal welfare is now an additional concern. The law no longer tries solely to prevent the maltreatment of animals by bad behavior. The concept of intrinsic value changes the question of animal protection from a question concerning the moral quality of certain forms of human behaviour (is it reasonable?), into a question concerning the protection of the animal itself. This makes it possible to discuss established practices in animal husbandry that are detrimental to the welfare of animals.

The discussion on animal biotechnology showed that the recognition of the intrinsic value of animals also had another implication. We are able to change the functioning of an animal, in such a way that we may take away the capacity to have certain experiences. The idea that we deprive animals from certain possible good experiences, without causing suffering, does not seem to fit in with the idea of "intrinsic value". In order to derive concrete criteria to assess whether such acts are problematic, we need concepts that go beyond animal welfare. In this discussion animal integrity is proposed as a criterion.

4. The function of "intrinsic value of animals"

The "intrinsic value of animals" was introduced in the sociopolitical debate in 1981 to establish a firm basis for improving the lives of animals under human custody. Despite the introduction of this key-concept in the legislative process and in parliamentary debate, this goal has only partly been reached. Although it seems to be the case that animal experiments are now much better assessed by independent committees, the situation of livestock did not improve (much).

4.1 The structure of the debate
In the sociopolitical debate so far, only two questions have been discussed: (1) whether or not (certain) animals should be protected and (2) in what way this protection has to be elaborated. The concept of "intrinsic value" of animals was originally introduced in the debate on the question *whether or not* entities (such as animals) are "proper objects of moral concern". Introduction of the concept in the memorandum *Rijksoverheid en Dierenbescherming* (National Government and Animal Protection) meant a change in point of departure for animal protection legislation. Since the Dutch government endorsed the intrinsic value of the individual animal as an explicit point of departure for its policy on human-animal relationship, legislation focused on the life of animals and not on concrete human acts. In the memorandum the term "intrinsic" is chosen because it is opposite to "instrumental". With "intrinsic value" is designated that animals have a value independent from their "instrumental" value to human beings. "Intrinsic value" is used to express that animals are not "mere things". This implies that for their own sake, their well-being should be taken into consideration: we are obliged not to impose suffering upon them, or at least not without sufficient justification. It seems that, as far as this first debate is concerned, we have reached consensus on the question whether animals are proper objects of moral concern.

This discussion is not uniquely Dutch. In the German-speaking world a similar discussion has developed under the heading of *Würde der Kreatur* (Teutsch 1995). And this idea has even been voted (by the plebiscite of May 1992) into the Swiss Federal Constitution. According to Article 24novies paragraph 3 BV., "the Swiss Confederation shall promulgate laws concerning the handling of germ cells and genotype of animals, plants and other organisms. In doing so it shall take into account the dignity of non-human organisms (Würde der Kreatur) as well as the safety of humans, animals and the environment, and protect the genetic diversity of animal and plant species". According to an expert opinion (Balzer et al. 1997) written on request of the Swiss Government, this means that the Swiss constitution is guided in Art. 24 novies Para 3 BV by a (limited) biocentric conception, where consequently not only humans but also animals and plants (and some other organisms) are worthy of moral consideration for their own sake".

Thus, "intrinsic value" expresses the idea that animals are not things, mere instruments or machines. This idea is broadly shared within our society.

The consensus reached in the first debate has consequences for the second debate. Having reached some consensus on animals as proper objects of moral concern, the question now arises *in what way* this concern has to be elaborated. The recognition of intrinsic value of animals changed the debate. Firstly, one can say that this common point of departure strengthened the already accepted idea of prevention of cruelty and maltreatment. The idea that cruelty towards animals is not acceptable has been expanded to all animals. Sport hunting has to defend itself against the reproach that it is done with "cruel intentions". This lies at the heart of the discussion on the Flora and Fauna Bill. The idea that animals should be protected against maltreatment expanded too. In order to protect animals against possible maltreatment (disproportionality) in animal experiments, the moral assessment of experiments has been taken out of the hands of those directly involved. Independent Animal Experiment Committees are now obligatory.

Since 1981, however, the prevention of certain human acts (cruel or disproportional) is no longer the sole purpose of the animal protection legislation. To this purpose is added the purpose of protecting of animals in certain housing systems. Protection against suffering beyond pain and injury is added. The law no longer tries solely to prevent the maltreatment of animals by bad behaving individuals. The consequences for animal life become more central as compared to the reasonableness of human behaviour. Established practices in animal husbandry that are detrimental to the welfare of animals become object of discussion. This has lead to the "no-unless"-structure of the Animal Health Welfare Act, which continually forces a judgement on the acceptability of a specific activity involving animals. By forcing one to consider the (moral and legal) admissibility of actions, the Act expresses the recognition of the intrinsic value of animals, but this recognition gives no concrete indication of how that should be put into practice. And in practice not much has changed.

4.2 Changing practice

This brings us to the third level of debate, namely the question *what weight* this moral concern has to have in concrete discussions? At what price (economical or moral) can we enforce our moral concern? In this debate we seem to have reached (until now) little societal consensus. Intrinsic value of animals is not helpful in increasing the level of consensus.

The reason that the debate on intrinsic value has not resulted in the improvement of the welfare of agricultural animals can be found in the institutional and economical arrangements of agriculture. Animal husbandry is an integrated part of agriculture. Changing the welfare of the animals seems hardly possible without changing the whole system. The structure of agricultural practice is such that it is not possible to improve animal welfare without reshaping its whole structure (Dubbink 1998). But changing the whole system is expensive. These changes have to be implemented in an economically highly competitive context. Agriculture and food-production are moving towards worldwide free trade. Changing such a system seems only possible with the help of an external force. Government should take the lead in changing agricultural practice. Government, however, can - under normal circumstances - not implement changes in a practice if the vast majority of those concerned are against it (Dubbink 1998). If government wants to change the practice, more is necessary.

An analysis of the recent discussion in Dutch Pig-industry makes this clear. In 1997 and in the first months of 1998 there was in the Netherlands an outbreak of classical swine fever. This outbreak was not limited to a small area. A ban on the export of pigs, meat and other products created a huge financial setback for the sector. In order to control this epidemic 10 million pigs, among which 4 million piglets, had to be killed. This caused a public unrest with the situation. A public campaign organized by Dutch writers against the current pig farming industry received much attention and support.

The outbreak of epizootic diseases in pig farming changed its image. The newspaper pictures of dead pigs, of crowded housing systems and the killing of piglets created public support for a change in the industry. Above this, it became clear that the environmental damage caused by the pig farming industry made stricter environmental regulations necessary. In order to understand the problems of Dutch Pig farming Industry some figures are helpful. In 1996 there were 22,000 farms with pigs, with an average of 635 animals: a total of 14,5 million animals in the Netherlands. The average pig density in the Netherlands is 330 animals per square kilometre, but the animals are concentrated in the south-east of the Netherlands. There the density is 1237 pigs per square kilometre (Fokkinga, 1997). In a letter to parliament the Minister of Agriculture proposed a restructuring of the pig farming industry, namely 25% reduction in pigs and the improvement of welfare (TK II 1996/97 25 448-1). These plans resulted in two proposals: the *Restructuring Pig Farming Act* and a Change in the *Pig regulations*, based upon the AHWA. The minister used the momentum created by the Classical Swine fever to change the structure of the pig farming industry. His proposals created a lot of unrest among farmers. These regulations were seen as unfair, unbalanced and unjustified. In parliament this lead to severe political discussions.

In these discussion the Council on Animal Matters played a role too. In a letter to Parliament of 15 November 1997 it criticized the welfare regulations. Firstly, it accepted the main goal of the regulations (Letter Council of Animal Matters): "The Council of Animal Matters agrees unanimously with the three basic points of the change in the *Pig Regulations*: group housing, stable groups and the enlargement of the floor space. The council has the conviction that these three basic point will improve animal welfare, *if they are implemented in the right way*." (italics added). However some members of the Council had 'practical objections' against immediate implementation. Their objections were: "If we change the *Pig Regulations* we have to do it properly. The, in principle, good starting points of the Change can fail in practice. In practice the farmers will tend to explore the margins. More consultation is necessary, also to increase acceptance". Political discussion forced the Minister to withdraw his proposed Change. This put the associated welfare improvements in the restructuring at risk. However, the Minister rapidly suggested new changes. Some practical changes were made, but the central ideas stayed the same. The *Restructuring Pig Farming Act* was accepted by parliament on 7 April 1998 and the Act and the second Change in the *Pig Regulations* have come in force in the autumn of 1998.

The second Change in the *Pig regulations* is, of course, not perfect. The possibility of farmers exploring the margins will not be excluded. It is, however, impossible to wait for a perfect regulation. By introducing these rules a fundamental choice is made: pigs are taken as point of reference in the way they are, as social animals. Housing systems need to be adapted to this fact, instead of adapting the animals to the housing system. After this fundamental choice, a new situation arises in which new welfare problems can be solved.

The legal means for the restructuring of the pig farming industry are ready and are being implemented. The industry, however, does not accept them. They consider the new acts as unjustified and unlawful. They challenge them in court because they consider the reduction of 25% an unjustified violation of their property rights. We do not yet know what the outcome of this judicial battle will be.

5. Conclusion

The concept of the intrinsic value of animals is one that is often used in moral discussions as a vague concept with a very persuasive function. It has opened a situation in which a legislative context may improve animal life. It even strengthened already accepted ideas of prevention of cruelty and maltreatment of animals. It added a purpose to animal protection legislation: to protect animals in established practices in animal husbandry that are detrimental to animal welfare. The "no-unless"-structure of the *Animal Health Welfare Act* provides a legal framework for this.

Implementation of this framework, however, has only contained the animal welfare situation on a certain level. This seems not enough. It can, however, function as a point of departure for further improvement. Concrete improvement of animal lives depends on the reconstruction of animal husbandry: the development of housing-systems that enable sustainable animal husbandry with acceptable levels of animal welfare.

What does this mean for the socio-political debate? The recognition of the intrinsic value of animals in the policy documents referred to above was not simply an idea trumped up by a few civil servants, but reflected a growing public awareness that man cannot simply do with animals whatever he pleases, that animals have an importance and value, irrespective of the importance or value they have for us: in short, that animals have moral status. This moral awareness subsequently obtained its most direct statutory expression in the *Animal Health and Welfare Act*. This Act by design requires that all human behaviour towards animals should at least also be appraised from the perspective of the animals. The welfare chapter in particular, in which a "no unless"-policy is prescribed, continually forces a judgement on the acceptability of a specific activity involving animals. By forcing one to consider the (moral and legal) admissibility of actions, the Act does give expression to the recognition of the intrinsic value of animals, but as indicated above, this recognition gives no direct indication of how that should be put into practice. For the discussion on the *Flora and Fauna Bill*, this implies that the right place for the recognition of the intrinsic value of animals in the Act is in the preamble.

Notes

[1] The author would like to express special thanks to Marleen Houpt of the Ministry of Agriculture, Nature Management and Fisheries, and Ronno Tramper and Jan Vorstenbosch of the Centre for Bio-ethics and Health Law. Parts of this text have been presented at the Netherlands School for Research in Practical Philosophy. The research for this paper was partly done as a post-doc in the pionier-project "Ideals in Law, Morality and Politics" of the Schoordijkinstituut for Jurisprudence (Tilburg University) and was financially supported by the Netherlands Organisation for Scientific Research (NWO).
[2] On 29 September and 2 October 1997: Kamerstukken (Parliamentary Documents) II, 1997/1998: 23147, 23580-112, and Handelingen van de Tweede Kamer (Proceedings of the Lower House), 2 Oct. 1997, TK 9-591 to 625.
[3] This analysis is partly based upon: Boon 1983; Davids 1989 ; Brom 1997a; and Dubbink 1998.

Literature

- Advisory Committee (1990). *Ethics and Biotechnology in Animals*, Report by the Advisory Committee Ethics and Biotechnology in Animals. Wageningen: NRLO.
- Balzer, P., Rippe K-P. & Schaber P. (1997). *Was heisst Würde der Kreatur?* Gutachten für das Bundesamt für Umwelt, Wald und Landschaft, Schriftenreihe Umwelt nr. 294. Bern: BUWAL.
- Boon, D. (1983). *Nederlands Dierenrecht*. Arnhem: Gouda Quint (Thesis Groningen University).
- Boon, D. (1985). *Een wet voor het welzijn van dieren*, voorbereid door Dirk Boon. 's-Gravenhage, Nederlandse Vereniging tot Bescherming van Dieren.
- Brambell-report (1965). *Report of the technical committee to inquire into the welfare of animals kept under intensive husbandry systems*. London: HMO.
- Brom, F.W.A. (1997a). *Onherstelbaar verbeterd. Biotechnologie bij dieren als een moreel probleem*. Assen: Van Gorcum (Thesis Utrecht University).
- Brom, F.W.A. (1997b). Animal welfare, public policy and ethics, in: M.Dol et al. (eds), *Animal consciousness and animal ethics. Perspectives from the Netherlands*. (pp. 208222), Assen: Van Gorcum.
- Brom F.W.A. & Schroten, E. (1993). Ethical questions around animal biotechnology. The Dutch approach. *Livestock Production Science,* 36, 99-107.
- Brom F.W.A. & Schroten, E.(1998). Ethics and animal biotechnology. An analysis against the background of public policy in the Netherlands. *Animal Issues*, 2 (2), 37-50.
- Bruil, D.W. (1997). Fundamentele rechten voor dieren, in: J.P. Loof & P.B. Cliteur, *Mensenrechten, dierenrechten en ecosysteemrechten*. Leiden: NCJM 20, 87-89.
- Cock Buning, Tj. de (1996). Limitations of the Contribution of Ethics Committees to Public Debate, R. von Schomberg, P. Wheale (ed), *The social management of biotechnology: workshop proceeding*. Tilburg: Faculty of Philosophy, 61-72.
- Council for Animal Matters, Brief van de Raad voor Dierenaangelegenheden aan de Voorzitter van de Vaste Kamercommissie voor Landbouw, Natuurbeheer en Visserij van 04-12-1997.
- Davids, K. (1989). *Dieren en Nederlanders*. Utrecht: Matrijs.
- Dubbink, W. (1998). Dieren, Dienders en Democratie. *Kennis en methode*, 314-338.
- Fokkinga, A. (1997).*Het Varken*. Bussum: TOTH.
- Harrison R. (1964). *Animal machines: the new factory farming industry*. London: V. Stuart.
- Reenen, C.G. van, Blokhuis H.J. (1993). Investigating welfare of dairy calves involved in genetic modification: problems and perspectives, *Livestock Production Science* 36, 81-90.
- Russel, W.M.S., Burch R.L. (1959). *The Principles of Humane Experimental Techniques*. London: Methuen.
- Schmidt, H.J. (1891). *Geschiedenis van het Wetboek van strafrecht. Volledige verzameling van regeeringsontwerpen, gewisselde stukken, gevoerde beraadslagingen enz.* Bijeengebracht en gerangschikt door H.J. Schmidt. Herzien en aangevuld met de wijzigingen door J.W. Schmidt, Tweede Deel. Haarlem: Tjeenk Willink.
- Schroten, E. (1998). The "Herman Case": The usefulness of the Wide Reflective Equilibrium Model for Ethics Committees, in: W. van der Burg & T. van Willigenburg (eds). *Reflective Equilibrium. Essays in Honour of Robert Heeger* (pp. 219-229), Dordrecht: Kluwer Academic Publishers.

- Teutsch, G.M. (1995). *Die 'Würde der Kreatur'. Erläuterungen zu einem neuen Verfassungsbegriff am Beispiel des Tieres*. Stutgart: Haupt.
- Verhoog, H. (1992). Ethics and genetic engineering of animals, in: A.W. Musschenga, B. Voorzanger, A. Soeteman (eds.), *Morality, Worldview and Law; The Idea of a Universal Morality and its Critics* (pp. 267-278). Assen: Van Gorcum.
- Witsen, H.M. (1888). *Rechtskundige beschouwingen over vivisectie*. Amsterdam: Thesis Gemeentelijke Universiteit.

Intrinsic value & the struggle against anthropocentrism

Edward van der Tuuk

In this contribution I will reflect on the concept of intrinsic value by highlighting some of the recent developments in the field of biotechnology. Subsequently, I will analyze some current views on the relationship between modern biotechnology and the intrinsic value of the animal. Finally, I will evaluate some of the issues to which intrinsic value relates.

1. The moral status of animals in The Netherlands from 1880 to 1980

In the first contribution to this volume it was outlined how moral attitudes towards animals (as expressed in public debate and legislation) changed over time. Until recently, the use of animals was regulated by prohibiting those activities that were regarded as offensive to humans (the socalled principle of offence) or at odds with human dignity. These regulations were anthropocentric in character: their objective was to protect the moral feelings and values of human individuals. Other forms of legislation concerning animals sprang from agricultural, economical and veterinary motives.

During the second half of the twentieth century, the intensification of cattle-breeding and the increased use of laboratory animals provoked fierce debates in which the negative consequences for the animals *themselves* became an issue. Notably during the sixties and seventies, pressure groups started to argue on behalf of the interests of animals kept in laboratories and farms. They expressed their discontent with laws that prohibited deliberate cruelty to animals only insofar as feelings of human individuals were offended or the cruelty involved could be regarded as a defamation on human dignity. They called for new forms of legislation that would protect animals for non-anthropocentric reasons. In these discussions (the moral relevance of the animal's welfare) two key issues were involved. To begin with, the harm principle, rather than the offense principle, should be the moral foundation for the protection of animals. Secondly, as to the skepticism expressed by scientists regarding the presence of consciousness and self-awareness in animals, they should be granted the benefit of the doubt by adopting the so-called analogy postulate. Applied ethological research into the behaviour of animals in captivity made it clear that the intensive use of animals had negative effects on the animal's health and well-being. Nevertheless, concern for the well-being of animals had to be purged from anthropomorphism and sentimentalism. This point of view is taken for example in a report by the *Federation of*

Veterinarians in the EEC (FVE, 1978) concerning welfare-problems among domestic animals. This document states that although the interests of animals often conflict with the demands of society, society remains responsible for the welfare of the animals involved. Considerations regarding animal welfare ought to be based on veterinary, scientific and ethological norms, but not on sentiment. And although animals do not have fundamental rights, human beings have certain moral obligations towards them. These statements indicated the extend to which the concern for animal welfare became increasingly independent from preoccupations with decency. The harm suffered by the animal became point of departure. Now that not only the interests and values of human individuals counted, but also the interests of the animals themselves, animal protection had become less anthropocentric.

During the seventies and eighties, the criticism regarding the living conditions of farm and laboratory animals became mixed up with other social debates, notably the discussions concerning the protection of the (natural) environment and the ones concerning the development of new breeding techniques. Due to this broadening of the issues, other objections against the use of animals for scientific or economic reasons emerged. The instrumental use of the animals, it was said, is hard to reconcile with their intrinsic (or inherent) value. In 1981 the Dutch government included the intrinsic value-argument in a statement concerning the protection of animals (CRM 1981). Now a principle was formulated that allowed for the possibility that, in some cases, the interests of animals might prevail over and above those of science and industry. The interests of the animal involved health and well-being as experienced by the animals themselves, independent from considerations concerning their suitability for human use. It was now claimed that animals have intrinsic value, that is, a good of their own, and an interest in their own well-being. This value is inalienable, closely linked to the life of the animal, and it continues to exist as long as the animal is alive (Boon 1986). Whereas animal interests tended to be underestimated by the traditional "offence principle", and overestimated by the concept of animal rights, the concept of intrinsic value is situated between both extremes. Thus, it may enable us to open up and further explore the ethical issue of animal interest.

2. Recent social and bio-technological developments

The concern for environmental issues and the critical attitude towards certain breeding techniques were already mentioned as factors that broadened the scope of the debate on the moral status of animals in captivity. Recent developments within the field of biotechnology constituted yet another factor. After the commotion concerning the transgenic bull Herman and the celebrated lactoferrine-project of Genepharming, modern biotechnology has almost become a synonym for genetic engineering. In the debate on Herman, concern for the intrinsic value of animals became an issue in its own right. Many participants felt that there was more to intrinsic value than merely the concern for the animal's welfare. Since then, intrinsic value not only refers to the animal's welfare, but also to the moral attitude society takes towards animals as such.

This is clearly reflected in the Health- and Welfare Act on Animals (1994), that regulates the use of animals and aims at protecting animals for their own sake. Article 66 defines two conditions under which the Minister of Agriculture may forego the application of biotechnology to animals: (a) unacceptable consequences for the health and well-being of the animals, and (b) ethical objections, where the latter phrase refers to considerations concerning the intrinsic value of the animal. Other recent developments in the field of biotechnology (such as cloning experiments, xenotransplantation, etcetera), also had an impact on public debate. Issues such as generic boundaries, species integrity, naturalness and the place of mankind in the natural order of things, became increasingly associated with the issue of intrinsic value. Concern for intrinsic value may even conflict with a concern for animal welfare. For example: is it allowed to use biotechnologies like genetic modification in order to combat animal diseases, like for example mastitis (an affection of the udder, caused by the intensive milking of cows)? A business manager from *(Gene)Pharming* once stated that, in such a case, it would be unethical not to use these techniques. Suppose it would be possible to eliminate some of the negative effects of intensive breeding, or of the use of laboratory animals for experimentation, by adjusting the animals involved to their artificial surroundings, using genetic modification, instead of adjusting the practices involved to the natural needs of animals - would that be ethically objectionable? What do we precisely mean when we say that genetic engineering is harmful to animals? Is it reasonable to impose restrictions on certain animal practices if harm to animals in the strict sense is not involved? Can the appeal to intrinsic value provide us with a reason for doing so? It all depends on how we interpret this term.

3. Differing views on intrinsic value

The concept of intrinsic value can be regarded as an intellectual instrument in the struggle against anthropocentrism (Musschenga 1994). Nevertheless, several views on the meaning of "intrinsic value" can be distinguished. The emphasis on intrinsic value results from the intensification of the way animals are being used and instrumentalized, especially during the last decades. Most advocates of the intrinsic value of animals will use it as the conceptual opposite to "instrumental value" - i.e. the economical value an animal has for us, its usefulness. The animal is of value for its own sake. It is not a mere thing. The difficult question then is, whether or not these values, in order to be called "intrinsic", must exist independent of the one who does the valuing. On the one hand it is claimed that, as *we* are the ones that attribute value to animals, this value does not exist "out there". And therefore, intrinsic value is not the proper term. The value of the animal, whether instrumental, moral, aesthetical, or other, is always an attributed one. On the other hand, however, it is claimed that man is not the measure of all things, and that the most crucial aspect of intrinsic value consists precisely in the fact that it is not an *attributed* value, but an *objective* one, something belonging to the animal itself. According to G.E. Moore, intrinsic value refers to the value things would have if they existed by themselves, in absolute isolation. It is a value that depends on the *non-relational properties* of something (rarity, for example, would be a relational property - Moore 1903/1952, p. 187; cf. Musschenga 1994). And Tom Regan likewise states that "the presence of inherent value in a natural object is independent of any awareness, interest, or appreciation of it by any conscious being" (cited in (for example) Bracke 1990, p. 46, Achterberg & Zweers 1986, p. 128). Otherwise, they argue, anthropocentrism would not be overcome. Yet, it is important not to confuse antropo*centric* with anthropo*genic* values. An anthropogenic value is a value *generated* by humans beings, whereas an anthropocentric value implies that human interests are considered more valuable and more important than the interests of non-humans. As Achterberg (1992) pointed out, it is not necessary to maintain that intrinsic values really exist as objective properties, which intrinsically valuable entities would also have totally independent of a relation to a valuating subject. Avoiding both a subjectivistic and an objectivistic interpretation of "intrinsic value", I will now point out what an *anthropogenic* interpretation of the term implies.

4. Respect for intrinsic value - an anthropogenic view

Something which has intrinsic value ought to be respected because it has a special worth or meaning that transcends the preferences of the individual involved. Thus, intrinsic value can apply to persons, but also to objects of art, holy places, old buildings, geographical sites, animal species, etcetera. All things mentioned have a certain meaning beyond their usefulness, their instrumental value. They become sacred in a way, like monuments. We demand respect for things which are generally regarded as highly valuable and at that point, we enter the sphere of morality.

But not only entities can have this sort of intrinsic value, also certain properties can, like beauty, naturalness, wildness or complexity. Linskens, Achterberg and Verhoog have argued that the more species-specific characteristics of an animal have disappeared, the less reason we have to value the animal as an end in itself" (1990, p. 92-94). To the extent to which animals (either individuals or species) become increasingly artificial and dependent on our care, their intrinsic value will decrease (regardless of whether they are able to suffer or not).

The value of properties like wildness and naturalness is not actively (that is, subjectively) attributed, but rather passively respected. It entails a form of respect, an attitude of deference or awe. Thus, protection of animals is a way of civilizing people, as the slogan of the *Dutch Society for the Protection of Animals* phrases it. This is also the view which was advocated in the article that initially introduced the concept of intrinsic value in the Dutch debate. As an alternative to anthropocentrism and anthropomorphism, the writer proposes that humans must see themselves as part of living nature, a nature that has its own, intrinsic value, although man may play a special role as steward, a role connected with his task of becoming truly human (Verhoog 1980, 85). This attitude of respect generates moral objections, not only to genetic engineering itself, but also to the patenting of genetically modified organisms. The very idea of patenting entails a violation of the intrinsic value, not only of the organism involved, but of life in general.

This attitude of respect can be directed towards individual animals, species, biological processes, biotopes, geotopes, even to life as such. It is directed towards natural entities that have a *telos*, a good of their own. At this point, however, a distinction must be made between biocentrism and ecocentrism. Whereas biocentrism stresses the right of *individual* organisms to seek their own good, ecocentrism considers natural activity to be morally relevant in a more general way. As Colwell (1989) puts it, the inherent complexity of individual organisms, species, habitats, and ecosystems as centers of relations *independent of human will* merit our recognition of their intrinsic value and thus make us responsible for their appropriate care" (p. 34). This admiring stance towards nature, which is also expressed in Schweizer's dictum "reverence for life", is an *attitudinal* kind of respect for certain *valued properties*, such as complexity and independence.

Most animal protectionists, however, defend the rights and interests of *individual* animals. One reason for doing so is, that only individual animals can be *harmed* in the sense of experiencing pain. But biocentrists hold that all *teleological centres of life* can be harmed, simply by being disturbed or interfered with. One might object to this, however, by saying that only conscious creatures can be harmed, while other organisms can only be damaged, and natural processes can only be hindered or impeded. Since this form of respect is somehow related to the cultural meaning of an animal, it is more difficult to connect with actual properties of *individual* animals than considerations concerning animal welfare. For this reason, some authors propose to connect the term intrinsic value with words like "dignity" or "inherent worth", rather than with "attitudinal respect" (Heeger 1992, p. 252-261; Rutgers 1993, p. 99-100).

5. Intrinsic value as a formal basis for moral concern

As the intrinsic value of an individual animal is recognized, it becomes an object of moral concern - a moral patient. Whenever intrinsic value is recognized without referring to certain valued properties of the animal involved, the term "intrinsic value" is used in a *formal* sense. Intrinsic value then simply obliges moral actors to acknowledge the animal's interests. The term "interests", however, is as ambiguous as it is formal. I will not enter into this issue at length, but merely confine myself to the remark that the term "interest" always refers to certain needs or demands, that is, to certain properties of the animal itself that are real, rather than attributed. What the interests of the animal involved consist in, is not yet indicated by the term "intrinsic value". Rather, the actual interests have to be determined with the help of empirical knowledge. Only empirical knowledge will tell us what it is that can actually be harmed in the animal involved. Thus, anthropocentrism can only be avoided if we refrain from confusing certain valued properties that have special meaning for *us* (like beauty, biological complexity, etc.) with the needs and preferences, in short the interests, of the animal itself.

Furthermore, respect for intrinsic value can be interpreted in a more or less utilitarian, as well as in a more or less deontological manner. Singer's theory of equal consideration of interests or "species-impartiality", is an example of the utilitarian interpretation. The extent to which the animal constitutes an object of moral concern depends entirely on the number and intensity of its needs and preferences. We have more obligations towards very sentient animals than towards animals that are less sentient. Bracke, for example, argues that preference frustration is morally relevant only in the case of a conscious animal. Moral agents have the obligation to reduce the frustration of conscious preferences.

Although this utilitarian interpretation of intrinsic value can be regarded as non-anthropocentric insofar as it advocates equal consideration of interests, one may nonetheless argue that the moral value or status of the animal is still *attributed* by man. Others, however, like Regan for instance, try to go a step further. Although he distinguishes between (on the one hand) the animal's biological needs and (on the other hand) the animal's moral status, he maintains that *both* are intrinsic properties of the animal. More precisely, he argues that, whereas the *intrinsic value* of an animal is variable and dependent on its needs or interests, the *inherent value* of an animal is the value of the animal *as such*, of the animal as *subject-of-a-life*, as centre of its own universe and as generator of preferences (Regan 1983, 1979; cf. Bracke 1990, p. 44). According to Regan, inherent value is equally possessed by all subjects-of-a-life - and he adds that all mentally normal mammals of at least one year old must be regarded as such (1984, p. 77). Unlike "intrinsic value", that is, "inherent value" does not pertain to animals to a higher or lesser degree. An animal either has it, or not (Regan 1984, pp. 240-241; Cf. Tester 1991, p. 6). It exists independent of awareness, interest, or appreciation. If, on the other hand, one maintains that the moral status of animals depends on things like needs and preferences, this would mean that moral status is something which is attributed, that it is anthropogenic (i.e. generated by man).

Another deontological argument against the utilitarian interpretation is that utilitarian accounts are notoriously ill-suited when it comes to defending or acknowledging animal rights. Rather, utilitarianism implies that we can always overcome our obligations towards animals simply by increasing our interests in using them. Therefore, animal rights can only be based on inherent value and immediate (rather than calculated) respect. On behalf of utilitarianism, however, it must be pointed out that animals are granted a right to an equal consideration of interests. The crucial difference between the utilitarian and the deontological view on animal rights then seems to be that the first does not accept the existence of some sort of value "behind" the animal's actual needs or preferences. If we could adapt an animal to its artificial surroundings by genetically eliminating certain needs of preferences, for example, this would be a morally neutral intervention from a utilitarian point of view. Bracke (1990) rejects the view that animals have inherent value or fundamental rights (such a s the right not to be killed) by saying that they do not have "second order desires", that is: they do not know who or what they are and cannot question issues like life and death. Animals only have provisional rights. Verhoog, however, denies that intrinsic value has any direct bearing upon interests or rights. In his view, intrinsic value rather articulates an attitude of respect towards animals.

So on the one hand we have the view that the moral status of animals is linked to interests or other properties that can be measured by man, and on the other hand we have the view that the value of animals is not something that can be measured because it is a kind of dignity or worth, present somehow in the animal itself. The mere fact that the animal exists, is a rationale for its dignity and demands an attitude of respect. The weakness of the deontological approach resides in the fact that it cannot say much about the moral problems that arise in situations of conflict between the interests of animals in captivity and the interests of human beings who want to use them to some end. The weakness of the utilitarian approach is that it only allows us to speak about animals as the object of our actions. It does not say anything about wild animals beyond our reach. The issue of intrinsic value only comes up when the animal already has some kind of instrumental value.

6. Intrinsic value as an independent quality

In the discussion so far it became clear that intrinsic value refers to what makes an animal morally relevant, independent of its usefulness to man. Sometimes, the intrinsic value of an animal is connected with its *telos* - it is suggested that intrinsic value resides in the fact that the animal has a good of its own. "Telos" is an Aristotelian concept referring to the fact that animals strive to realize their natural ends. Genetic engineering, in this view, is highly problematic because it may affect the "telos" of the animal. This interpretation has much in common with Clark's concept of "self-realisation" and Regan's concept of "inherent value". All these interpretations refer to objective properties that entail a normative component. An organic unity striving for self-realisation *prima facie* demands respect. Another interpretation of intrinsic value, however, rather views the animal from a scientific (biological and/or ethological) perspective. In this conception, certain (non-moral) standards can be formulated concerning the animal's bodily functions and its interaction with the environment. Suffering can be defined as a discrepancy between the animal's actual condition and these standards. The animal's natural behaviour basically aims at to minimalizing this discrepancy. The greater the discrepancy, and the longer the animal remains incapable of reducing it, the more it suffers. Baerends (1973) calls these standards "expectancy-values". In this sense intrinsic value is a descriptive, rather than an anthropogenic term, and as such it has no moral dimension to it. It refers to preferences and needs of animals which, if satisfied, contribute to the animal's welfare, and which, if frustrated, leave the animal frustrated. The animal's mental state constitutes a balance between satisfaction and frustration. There is nothing "behind" interests, needs, and frustration. Thus, the objective is to translate (as completely as possible) moral problems into empirical questions.
One problem with this view is that considerable individual differences between animals (with regard to subjective awareness, for example) may occur, as well as between species. Does this mean that some individuals (or species) may have more intrinsic value than others? The question then becomes whether something like subjective awareness is scalable. Are the minds of animals somehow comparable? If this is the case, then it might for example be argued that the so-called higher animals (being more complex and more similar to man) must be respected more than "lower" animals. A possible objection to such a procedure is

that comparisons between, for example, lions and hares, or turtles and humans, seem to involve anthropocentrism or anthropomorphism. Not only because, ultimately, we are unable to know what goes on in an animal's mind, but also because subjective awareness already refers to a property that is primarily human. Instead of comparing animals, therefore, one could argue that *every* animal as such may suffer to a higher or lesser degree, within the boundaries of its own consciousness. Even lower animals may suffer more or less severely. The same goes for a concept like "telos". We cannot say that a lion has "more telos" than a turtle. The ultimate consequence of such a line of argument would be, however, that all animals, lions as well as turtles, or ants, are morally relevant *to the same degree* - and this must seem objectionable to many.

7. Conclusion

Basically, there are three kinds of respect associated with the term intrinsic value. *Attitudinal respect* for the intrinsic value of natural things refers to an attitude of deference and awe, but is not primarily concerned with interests, rights or duties. Rather, every being has its own interior, its self, its mystery, its numinous aspect, and to deprive any being of this sacred quality is to disrupt the total order of the universe (Fox 1988, p. 89; Verhoog 1991, p. 156). *Formal respect*, on the other hand, implies at least some concern with interests of animals, and will grant animals certain basic rights. Finally, *deontological respect* will focus on certain qualities inherently present in animals (such as the telos of the animal, the basic needs of animals, etc.). It is on these qualities that rights of animals are based and it is on the basis of these qualities that animals deserve our attention and care.

The problem with attitudinal respect is that it does not tell us whether, and to what extent, use can be made of animals. And this really *is* a problem, as we are already using animals intensively. Therefore, such an approach has at least to be supplemented by a formal one which focusses on interests (of animals, of society, etc.) and on the question of how precisely they can be balanced-off against one another. Whenever intrinsic value is associated exclusively with attitudinal respect, something valuable is lost, namely the function attributed to this concept by the Dutch government in 1981. It would only serve to indicate that certain human individuals, sharing this attitude of respect, have "ethical objections" to certain forms of biotechnology, and this would simply imply a rehabilitation of the principle of offence. The progress made over the last (say) forty years is valuable. If notions like interests, animal rights, and harm are ignored altogether, we are very likely to fall short of our responsibilities towards animals.

Some object to applying intrinsic value or even fundamental rights to animals, because it would degrade human dignity. Others fear that granting animals inalienable rights will make all forms of animal use immoral. Killing an animal would then become equivalent to murder. My contention is, however, that acknowledging the intrinsic value of animals does not affect the dignity of humans, at least not in a negative manner, because it precisely addresses the animal's *own* value. Nor does granting certain rights to animals necessarily mean that they have a right to *life, limb and liberty* (*self-determination*) in the Lockean sense. When granting captive animals *certain rights*, we are defining our own obligations towards them and express our responsibility towards animals - a responsibility that primarily concerns the suffering that results from our use of them.

Literature

- Achterberg (1992).*Humanisme zonder arrogantie*, also: *Partners in de natuur*, 1986.
- Baerends G.P. e.a. (1973). *Ethologie: de biologie van gedrag*; pudoc, Wageningen.
- Berry T. (1988). in Fox, 1988; 89, in Verhoog; in Egbert e.a, 1991, p. 156.
- Boon, D. (1986).*Nederlands Dierenrecht*; Gouda Quint b.v., Arnhem, p. 99.
- Bracke, M. (1990). Killing Animals; or why no wrong is done to an animal when killed painlessly; Utrecht, p. 46; note 37 and also in: Wouter Achterberg & Wim Zweers (1986) (red). *Milieufilosofie tussen theorie en praktijk; van ecologisch perspectief naar maatschappelijke toepassing*; Jan van Arkel, Utrecht, p. 128.
- Colwell, R.K. (1994).Natural and unnatural history; biological diversity and genetic engineering; in: *Scientists and their responsibilities*; W.R. Shea & B. Sitter (red.) Watson Publishing, Canton, 1989. p. 34; in: Musschenga.
- Linskens M., Achterberg, Verhoog H. (1990). *Het maakbare dier; ethiek en transgene dieren*; nota, p. 92-94.
- Moore G.E. (1994). Principia Ethica; Cambridge, 1952 (orig. 1903), p. 187, in: Musschenga. *Nota Rijksoverheid en Dierenbescherming*, (1981). CRM (Ministry of Culture, Recreation, and Environmental issues).
- Regan, T. 1983, 1979, in Bracke, 1990; p. 44.
- Regan, T. (1984) 240-241, in Tester, 1991; 6.
- Verhoog H. (1980). Dierproeven en bio-industrie: een vette kluif voor ethici, in *Filosofie en Praktijk I*, 74-85.

Part II

Intrinsic Value of animals:
Ethical Issues

3

Inherent worth and respect for animal integrity

Bart Rutgers & Robert Heeger

1. Introduction

In many moral discussions on the treatment of animals a reference is made to the 'intrinsic value of animals'. This phrase often expresses the belief that animals have *a value of their own*, a value that is independent of any instrumental value animals have for human welfare or happiness. This value is thought to be *important to morality*: in virtue of having a value of their own, animals are proper objects of moral consideration and such consideration is due to animals.

We would like to address two questions regarding this view. The first question concerns the clause that 'animals have a value of their own'. In discussions on animals and morality this clause is used ambiguously. How should the term 'a value of their own' be interpreted? We are seeking for an interpretation that makes the term effective for the task it is expected to fulfil: to offer a criterion, making it possible to answer the question whether moral consideration is due to animals or not. Three interpretations will be discussed: inherent value, intrinsic value, and inherent worth (section 2).

The second question that we wish to address concerns one of these interpretations: the concept of inherent worth. If one subscribes to the view that animals have inherent worth, one assumes a basic attitude of moral respect for them. Yet how should this attitude of respect be characterised? We propose to describe it as respect for animal integrity, and we shall put this description in concrete terms by considering some problematical cases from veterinary medicine and animal breeding (sections 3 and 4).

2. Three interpretations

This section concerns the meaning of the clause that 'animals have a value of their own'. We will discuss three interpretations of the term 'a value of their own', looking for an interpretation that is useful to answering the question whether moral consideration is due to animals or not (Heeger, 1992).

2.1. Inherent value
Many people hold that the value of animals should not be reduced to their usefulness, since animals are not only appreciated for their commercial value or utility. They evoke sympathy, astonishment and admiration, because they are as they are. Consequently, they should not be harmed, but instead cared for.

Companion animals have such a value for many people. Most owners have an affective relationship with their companion animals. Within such a relationship an animal is not being used as a tool for companionship, but people enter into the relation because of the animal itself. Wild animals provide another example. These animals may evoke feelings of wonderment and admiration. They are not simply appreciated for their utility, but for what they are. In both of these examples people tend to attribute value to animals because they appreciate them. This interpretation of the term 'a value of their own' could be called 'inherent value'. The value of animals, according to this interpretation, is wholly dependent on their being appreciated, and this appreciation necessarily rests on something inherent to them. 'Inherent' means that there are certain properties internally related to the animals that are appreciated, and 'dependent on their being appreciated' implies that animals will lose this value if they are no longer appreciated [1].

Could the concept of inherent value serve as a criterion if we want to answer the question of whether moral consideration is due to animals? For two reasons we believe that this concept is unsuitable for this purpose. Firstly, moral consideration is also due to those we do not appreciate. Moral consideration is not entirely dependent on the fact that someone or something enjoys appreciation. There are, for example, intensively farmed pigs that are seen as production units. However, that no inherent value is attributed to these pigs, does not imply that no moral consideration would be due to them. Secondly, moral consideration is not due to everything that we appreciate. Things can also have inherent value, for example, works of art, ancient monuments and nature reserves. The very fact that inherent value is attributed to a painting does not necessarily imply that we have moral duties *towards* it, that it is a proper object of moral consideration.

2.2. Intrinsic value

A very influential claim regarding animals and morality reads: Moral consideration is due to animals because they can suffer. By 'suffering' is meant enduring unpleasant emotional experiences. From that perspective, illness, disease or another physical disorder, and abnormal behaviour can be considered as manifestations of unpleasant experiences or frustrated interests. Animal suffering or abnormal behaviour are not only facts of which we take cognisance. They are also states, which have a negative value, for we bring them in relation to states we ourselves experience directly and value negatively. This relation is a reason for postulating: Animals can suffer or experience welfare, their interests can be frustrated or furthered, their suffering and the frustration of their interests are bad for themselves, and their welfare and the furtherance of their interests are good, desirable or valuable for themselves. This interpretation of the term 'a value of their own' may be called (negative and positive) 'intrinsic value'.

The concept of intrinsic value originally relates to events and states of affairs in the lives of *humans*. 'Positive intrinsic value' refers to events and states of affairs that people experience as pleasant for their own sake and that they value positively by virtue of their pleasantness; 'negative intrinsic value' stands for that which is experienced as unpleasant for its own sake and therefore valued negatively. The concept of intrinsic value may also refer to the interests that people strive for because they are worthwhile in themselves, and to the purposes that people try to achieve[2]. We must bear this in mind if we wish to apply the concept of intrinsic value to events and states of affairs in the lives of *animals*. It should be related to welfare or suffering experienced by animals and it should concern the furtherance or frustration of interests that are pursued by animals. If animals do not have the capacity to experience contentment, satisfaction, suffering or frustration, if they do not worry about what happens to them, and if they do not have desires, then the concept of intrinsic value does not apply to events or states of affairs in the lives of animals.

The concept of intrinsic value is in some ways appropriate to answering the question of whether moral consideration is due to animals. It enables us to give, for example, the following answer: We should have moral consideration for experiences of suffering and welfare, since morality includes a principle of beneficence and a principle of non-maleficence. According to these principles we ought to promote welfare and ought not to inflict suffering, irrespective of whether welfare or suffering is experienced by humans or animals. Experienced welfare and satisfaction are positive intrinsic values and suffering and frustration are negative intrinsic values. However, it should be noticed that according to this interpretation moral consideration is due only to *sentient* and *conscious* animals (the 'higher' animal species), and that moral consideration is due to these animals only insofar as suffering and experienced welfare is involved.

2.3. Inherent worth

To use the just mentioned concept of intrinsic value as a criterion for moral consideration is problematic for two reasons. Firstly, our moral intuitions can resist the claim that moral consideration is not due to animals that do not possess sentience or consciousness (the 'lower' animal species). Secondly, interferences in the lives of the 'higher' animals (to which nearly all domestic animals belong) may raise moral questions beyond suffering and welfare. For animals may be subjected to interferences that do not lead to actual suffering, or have no significant negative effects on the animals' health or welfare, but which are nonetheless morally objectionable. Examples of such treatments include ear-cropping in dogs, removing body parts, such as tails and genitals (castration/sterilisation), administering growth and production enhancers, genetic modification (e.g. Herman, the Dutch transgenic bull) and cloning (e.g. Dolly the sheep).

These examples show that there is a need for a normative criterion that reflects a sense of respect for animals beyond simply the care for their health and welfare. Such a normative criterion can be shaped by means of a theory on animals, which states that animals can be described as living beings with 'a good of their own' and 'interests of their own'.

By 'a good of their own' (or 'natural good'), we mean that animals have ends and purposes that are characteristic to them. They are oriented by themselves towards the development of species-characteristic abilities and the fulfilment of their needs. They strive to realise the patterns of behaviour specific to their species. They maintain the normal biological functions of their species by successfully adapting to their environment. They have some capacity for self-determination and self-renewal. It can be observed that it makes a difference to them whether or not their abilities can be manifested and it can meaningfully be stated that they are healthy or sick, that they are doing well (Von Wright, 1963; Taylor, 1986; Banner, 1995). This can further be clarified by stating that the own good of the animal refers to the capacities and functions that animals of the species in question are generally able to practise (Holland, 1990; Attfield, 1995).

The term 'interest' is used in a wide sense: animals have interests of their own because (and as far as) something can be detrimental or beneficial to them - in the sense that it makes a difference for their prospects and development – no matter whether they are conscious of it or not[3]. Only living beings, such as people and animals, can be better or worse off as a result of the actions or behaviour of other beings. If the term 'interest' is used in this wide sense, it can then be stated that animals have interests of their own because they have a good of their own. They have an interest in everything that contributes to the realisation of their good (Taylor, 1986; Achterberg, 1986, 1994).

It is possible to expertly judge what is beneficial or detrimental to the good of animals. However, expert judgements about the own good of animals do not answer the question of why the good of animals is morally important. This question can be answered as follows: we should have moral consideration for the good and the interests of animals because animals have inherent worth. That an animal has 'inherent worth' means the same as the following value judgement: a state of affairs where the good of the animal is realised, is better than a comparable state where this good is not realised or realised to a lesser degree[4].

The term 'inherent worth' expresses a substantial claim: the animal's intactness and its species-specific capacities and functions constitute a value towards which an attitude of moral respect is appropriate. Can the concept of inherent worth serve as a criterion, making it possible to answer the question whether moral consideration is due to animals? This depends on whether we recognise the claim that animals as living beings with a good of their own ought to be respected. Whether this claim will find our assent, has to do with our fundamental attitude towards life and the world. This fundamental attitude is linked to our view of life. The moral claim of respect is part of the philosophy of life held by many. We realise that, as human beings, we are part of the biological and ecological network to which all living beings belong and we are compelled to acknowledge that, in a good life, there is sufficient room for the quality of animal lives. Such a philosophy of life can be termed 'biocentric'.

From a biocentric point of view, inherent worth is ascribed to all members of the biotic community of a natural ecosystem. However, two points should be made in this context. That inherent worth is ascribed to animals (and other living beings) does not necessarily imply that all living beings are ascribed the same worth, whether they are a chimpanzee or a bush. A moderate biocentrism, in contrast to a radical biocentrism, allows for gradation. Consideration can be given to the fact that living beings differ in terms of their capacities and functions and that there are more significant obligations towards some beings than towards others. Moreover, that animals (and other living beings) have inherent worth does not mean that they are entitled to an absolute value. In contrast to a radical biocentrism, under a moderate biocentrism it is permissible to weigh up the inherent worth of an animal against another value, such as the health of humans. This kind of moderate biocentrism better conforms to our well-considered intuitions than any radical form of biocentrism.

3. Respect for animal integrity

In the previous section three interpretations of the term 'a value of their own' were discussed. We have sought an interpretation, which could serve as a criterion, making it possible to answer the question of whether moral consideration is due to animals. The concept of inherent value implies that animals have a value independent of their utility. However, it is not suitable as a criterion because it would be counter-intuitive to make moral consideration entirely dependent on the appreciation that someone or something (for example an animal) happens to enjoy. The concepts of intrinsic value and inherent worth are suitable to serve as criteria for moral consideration, but they differ with regard to the question of *which* moral consideration is due to animals. 'Intrinsic value' refers to suffering and experienced welfare, whereas 'inherent worth' has to do with the own good of living beings. The concept of inherent worth implies that an attitude of moral respect is appropriate towards living beings with a good of their own. In this section we shall address the question of how this attitude of respect should be characterised. Regarding animals we propose to describe it as respect for animal integrity.

We define animal integrity as follows: the wholeness and completeness of the animal and the species-specific balance of the creature, as well as the animal's capacity to maintain itself independently in an environment suitable to the species (Rutgers, 1993; Rutgers *et al.*, 1996; Grommers, 1997). This definition is made up of three mutually linked and complementary elements: (1) the wholeness and completeness, (2) the balance in species specificity, and (3) the capacity to independently maintain itself. It is essential that all three elements are satisfied for there to be a state of integrity.

According to the definition, integrity refers to both the individual animal and the species. One can speak of the integrity of the individual animal because every individual animal is a clearly defined biological entity with its own disposition. The development and course of life of the individual animal is determined by this disposition. The disposition of the individual animal is determined, for the most part, by the characteristics and qualities of the species to which the animal belongs. Every individual animal must be viewed as a specimen of its species. Species-characteristic integrity is understood to refer to the entirety of characteristics and qualities typical of a species. A discussion of species-characteristic integrity is of practical significance because a command or loss of certain species-specific qualities is not always discernible in an isolated individual. This includes, for example, social behaviour, such as the nurturing of offspring by a mother animal, or social relations between animals in a group. Species-specific characteristics serve here as a frame of reference for the disposition of the individual animal (as a specimen of its species).

Respect for animals (as living beings with a good of their own) expresses a moral obligation to consciously refrain from specific interferences in the lives of animals. Referring to our definition of animal integrity, this implies that man: (1) should not interfere with the wholeness and completeness of the animal, (2) should not disrupt the species-specific balance, and (3) should not deprive animals of the ability to maintain themselves independently in an environment suitable to the species. Infringement or violation of integrity therefore relates to these three criteria. Yet what does this description mean in concrete terms? In the following subsections we will consider some problematic cases from veterinary medicine and animal breeding in the light of these three criteria.

3.1. Physical interferences

People interfere in the lives of domestic animals for various different reasons. Physical interferences may take place with the purpose of adapting the animal to the owner's wishes. This type of physical interferences is called 'utility surgery'. Examples include tail-docking in dogs, horses, pigs, sheep and cattle, ear-cropping in dogs, removal of vocal chords in noisy dogs ('debarking'), removal of the claws of destructive cats ('declawing'), beak-trimming in chickens and ducks and dehorning of cattle, sheep and goats.

However, what makes utility surgery morally problematic? Tail-docking, ear-cropping, debarking, declawing, beak-trimming or dehorning are not only problematic because of the possible negative consequences for animal health and welfare. These procedures may be morally objectionable even if they do not lead to actual suffering or have no significant negative effects on the animal's health or welfare. Utility surgery is also morally problematic from the perspective of respect for animal integrity. One of the elements of animal integrity is wholeness and completeness (1st criterion). According to this criterion, respect for animal integrity implies that an animal is left whole, undamaged and intact. This means, among other things, that body parts should not be removed. Violation of the wholeness and completeness merely for economic or aesthetic reasons is incompatible with respect for animal integrity.

In the light of respect for animal integrity, is there any difference between utility surgery and surgical procedures for which a veterinary-medical necessity exists? There is in fact an important difference. Respect for animal integrity refers to human actions and people act with a specific goal or intention. This intentionality of human actions is taken into account in the concept of respect for integrity. Physical interference for which a veterinary-medical necessity exists must not be interpreted as an infringement of integrity, since the intention is to promote animal health and welfare. Such interference takes place in the (vital) interest of the animal. Examples include intestinal operations or the surgical removal of a tumour. It is therefore equally inappropriate to speak of infringement of integrity if a drug is administered to an animal with a veterinary-medical purpose. It would be strange if a vaccination or a therapeutic treatment were to be interpreted as a violation of integrity. In conclusion, if an action on an animal is performed on veterinary-medical grounds, that is to say that the action is aimed at promoting animal health and welfare or is intended to contribute to the restoration of the animal's biological intactness, this course of action should not be regarded as a violation of integrity. In contrast to surgical procedures that are (veterinary) medically indicated, utility surgery can indeed be said to be a violation of integrity because the intention is utterly different. In the context of utility surgery, removal of body parts is aimed at adapting the animal to the owner's desires. Infringement of the wholeness and completeness of the animal merely for economic or aesthetic aims should be regarded as a violation of integrity.

3.2. Animal breeding

Nearly all farm and companion animals kept or bred by people are domesticated animals. Domestication is generally understood as separating animals from their natural environment and keeping them under selective breeding conditions. This results in selection and breeding being determined by man. The purpose of domestication is to safeguard or increase the utility of animals for human needs. The breeding of dogs and cats, for instance, is aimed at producing animals with the breed characteristics, as regards appearance and behaviour that people desire. The breeding of farm animals is aimed at animals that, from an economic and biological viewpoint, will be able to produce as efficiently as possible.

Although domestication implies the instrumental use of animals, it is not necessarily in itself an infringement of integrity. Whether or not integrity comes into play depends upon the question of whether the three criteria of the integrity concept have sufficiently been met. The most important aspect of animal integrity is the preservation of species-specific abilities of self-regulation and self-maintenance, within an individual or a population, in an environment suitable to the species. This does not necessarily need to be the natural environment. Although domestication has brought about great changes in the living conditions of animals, the majority of domestic animals have appeared able to successfully adapt to changing conditions and to a large extent retain their species-specific characteristics in the process. The ability of animals to adapt is strongly connected to the high degree of flexibility in their species-specific traits, such as anatomy, physiology and behaviour. Infringement of integrity only occurs if, due to human interference, physical intactness is affected (1st criterion), the balance of the species specificity is disturbed (2nd criterion) or the animal loses its ability to independently maintain itself in an environment suitable to the species (3rd criterion). Thus, what forms of animal breeding must be considered an infringement of integrity, according to these criteria? We shall illustrate this below with some examples.

One clear example is the breeding of double-muscled cattle. Breeds of the double-muscled phenotype clearly deviate from non-double-muscled cattle breeds in a number of aspects, such as exceptional muscle development and a narrow pelvis. This causes serious parturition problems, which render Caesarean sections inevitable.

Why is the breeding of double-muscled cattle morally problematic? A morally important fact is that parturition problems cause animal suffering. According to the principle of non-maleficence, one ought not to inflict suffering on animals. Veterinarians, who take this moral principle seriously, opt for a Caesarean section to prevent needless suffering. However, animal suffering is not the only moral argument. The breeding of double-muscled cattle is also morally problematic in view of respect for animal integrity. Integrity is at issue because the criteria regarding the species-specific balance and the animals' ability to maintain themselves independently are not fulfilled. The excessively heavy musculature in conjunction with a narrow pelvis upsets the biological balance to such a degree that the cows are no longer able to calve normally and naturally. This deprives the cows of an essential ability in their existence as cattle. Through deliberate breeding of heavy calves, the cattle are no longer capable of independently maintaining themselves. Both disrupting the species-specific balance of the cow (2nd criterion) and depriving cows of their ability to maintain themselves independently (3rd criterion) is not compatible with respect for animal integrity.

As stated earlier, parturition problems in doubled-muscled cattle breeds have led to a large increase in Caesarean sections. It should be emphasised that the infringement of integrity does not take place at the moment of performing the Caesarean section. It is clear that a Caesarean section must be performed if it proves to be the only way to save the lives of both cow and unborn calf. In fact, because of his professional duty, a veterinarian can not refuse to perform a Caesarean section. Violation of animal integrity occurs at the moment of the choice of the bull, since the cattle breeder knowingly selects a bull that propagates heavy calves. He deliberately runs the risk of having to have a Caesarean section performed. Paving the way for parturition problems that necessitate a Caesarean section must be considered a violation of integrity.

Similar to the breeding of double-muscled cattle is the breeding of pedigree dogs, whereby the animals' ability to maintain themselves is lost because of strongly deviating conformation and function. Familiar examples are the English and French Bulldog. The large chest and narrow pelvis - both traits of the breeding standard - inevitably lead to parturition problems. A Caesarean section is almost always necessary. Without this operation, these breeds would soon die out.

Another problematic example of animal breeding is broiler chicken production. Broilers are bred for rapid growth to such an extent that 2 to 10 per cent of chicks in poultry farms literally grow to death. By focusing breeding methods on the capacity of the animal to put on as much muscle tissue as possible in a short period of time, the physiological balance is upset to such a degree that the animals die spontaneously. This method of broiler poultry production is not only morally problematic due to the negative consequences for health and welfare of the chickens, but also – and in particular – because the second criterion of the integrity concept is at issue. By disrupting the species-specific balance to such a degree, the chickens are deprived of the ability to lead normal and natural lives. This is not in accordance with respect for animal integrity.

3.3. Reproduction techniques

In breeding programmes, 'genetically excellent' animals are used for selection. These are animals with a specific heredity for desired features: breed traits in companion animals and production traits in farm animals. Natural mating is predominantly used for companion animals, while artificial reproduction techniques (particularly artificial insemination) are primarily employed for farm animals. The advantage of these artificial reproduction techniques is that breeding goals can more quickly be realised. To date the reproduction technique most commonly applied in the breeding of farm animals is artificial insemination, followed at a distance by embryo transfer. Developments in the field of biotechnology have led to new possibilities. By cloning embryos or adult animals, genetically identical animals can be created. Besides, it is possible to alter the genetic make-up of animals (genetic modification) by means of the recombinant-DNA technology in such a way, that animals with special or very specific production characteristics can be produced.

However, are these reproduction techniques problematic in the light of respect for animal integrity? This depends on the extent to which the three criteria of the integrity concept are fulfilled. Integrity is at issue with all reproduction techniques as far as functioning independently (3rd criterion) is concerned. The breeding process is becoming more technologised, particularly in the context of the more recent reproduction techniques. The natural reproduction process is replaced by a series of technological procedures, some of which, moreover, take place outside the body. By 'externalising' the reproduction process, the animal is deprived of its ability to reproduce independently and in a manner common to the species; it is as if the animal is 'dispossessed' of the natural reproduction process. Thus, it is the 'externalisation' of the reproduction process that makes reproduction techniques problematic from the perspective of respect for animal integrity.

All reproduction techniques, whether they involve artificial insemination, embryo transfer, cloning or genetic modification, involve externalisation of the reproduction process. However, the degree of externalisation is considerably smaller with artificial insemination than with, for example, cloning and genetic modification. We may therefore state that the more externalisation progresses, the more serious the integrity violation may be.

With respect to animal integrity, genetic modification involves more than a mere externalisation of the reproduction process. This can be illustrated with the example of transgenesis. Transgenesis is a technique by which a gene foreign to the species is added to an animal's genome. By introducing a gene foreign to the species to a gamete, the wholeness and completeness of the animal (first criterion of the integrity concept) is altered at its most fundamental level, the genome.

The fact that transgenesis implies an interference in the genetic intactness does not say anything about the seriousness of the violation of integrity. This depends on the extent to which the three criteria of the integrity concept are violated. The more the animal loses of its species-specific capacities and characteristics, the more serious the integrity violation. Examples of a serious integrity violation would be the bringing about of pigs, by means of genetic modification, that do not have the need to root or chickens without the need for ground-scratching.

3.4. Gradation of integrity violations

Is respect for animal integrity a sufficiently practicable criterion? For two reasons it might be argued that it is not. Firstly, integrity might be considered a yes/no criterion that cannot be understood gradually, that is to say, in terms of fewer or greater serious infringements. Secondly, one might think that integrity is a notion that is difficult to operationalise. These arguments are intertwined with each other. We have tried to demonstrate, with practical examples, that it is possible to evaluate violations of integrity not only in terms of yes or no – integrity is either violated or not – but also in terms of fewer or greater serious infringements. The seriousness of the infringement of integrity is determined by the extent of transgression of the three criteria of the integrity concept: the wholeness and completeness, the balance in species specificity, and the animals' capacity to independently maintain themselves in an environment suitable to the species. These elements relate to biological traits that are characteristic of the species in question. It can be objectively assessed by observation whether and, if so, to what degree, these biological characteristics are at issue. Integrity is an operational notion by virtue of this possibility of objective assessment. If there are doubts as to the extent or seriousness of the infringement of integrity in a specific situation, a test could be carried out. For example, by placing cattle in an environment suitable to the species, it can be shown experimentally that double-muscled cattle have largely lost the capacity to maintain themselves.

4. Conclusions

We have discussed three interpretations of the clause that animals have 'a value of their own': inherent value, intrinsic value and inherent worth. Two of them, intrinsic value and inherent worth seem suitable to answer the question of whether moral consideration is due to animals. Yet these interpretations differ in two respects. Firstly, while intrinsic value is attributable only to sentient and conscious animals, inherent worth can be ascribed to all animals. Secondly, while intrinsic value only refers to suffering and experienced welfare, inherent worth relates to the animals' good of their own and to the realisation of this good. We have tried to find criteria for moral consideration that encapsulate many considered judgements regarding the treatment of animals. We hold that one should not confine oneself to intrinsic value, but that one should also take inherent worth into account.

Inherent worth is related to a basic attitude of moral respect. We propose to describe this attitude as respect for animal integrity. This implies that people should not interfere with the wholeness and completeness of animals, should not disrupt the species-specific balance, and should not deprive animals of the ability to maintain themselves independently in an environment suitable to the species. We have tried to demonstrate that these criteria play an important role when moral issues that go beyond animal suffering and welfare have to be resolved.

To have and to display a basic attitude of moral respect for animals could be said to be to regulate one's conduct in conformity to a moral principle of respect for animal integrity. We would like to add two final remarks on this principle. Firstly, we would like to emphasise that respect for animal integrity does not imply that every infringement of integrity is unacceptable. In this connection, an analogy can be drawn to the principle of non-maleficence. This principle states that one ought not to inflict suffering on animals or harm their health and welfare, unless more weighty considerations oppose this. A similar rationale applies to the principle of respect for animal integrity: the integrity of the animal should not be violated unless the infringement can be justified on good moral grounds. Secondly, we want to point out that the principle of respect for animal integrity is not meant to replace the principles of beneficence and non-maleficence, but to be used in addition to those principles. Since respect for animal integrity has a different meaning than caring for the health and welfare of the animals, the principle of respect has an independent position in moral decision making.

Note

This inquiry was supported by the National Research Programme Ethics and Policies, which is subsidized by the Netherlands Organisation for Scientific Research (NWO) and the Ministry of Education, Culture and Science, the Ministry of Health, Welfare and Sport, and the Ministry of Agriculture, Nature Management and Fisheries.

Notes

1. This term has a different meaning than 'inherent value' in Regan (1984, 235-265). We instead define it with reference to Lewis (1946, chapter 13 & 14), Frankena (1979, 3-20, 13, 20) and Taylor (1986, 73-74).
2. This definition corresponds with what in ethics generally is meant by the term 'intrinsic value'; see e.g. Frankena (1973, 80-83, 89-92).
3. Thus, interest in the wide sense differs from interest in the narrow sense as being used in connection with the concept of intrinsic value (see section 2.2).
4. This definition makes use of an idea developed by Taylor (1986, 75).

Literature

- Achterberg, W. (1986). *Partners in de natuur.* Utrecht: Van Arkel.
- Achterberg, W. (1994). *Samenleving, natuur en duurzaamheid.* Assen: Van Gorcum
- Attfield, R. (1995). Genetic Engineering: Can Unnatural Kinds Be Wronged?, in P. Wheale & R. McNally (Eds), *Animal Genetic Engineering: Of Pigs, Oncomice and Men..* London: Pluto Press.
- Banner, M. (1995). *Report of the Committee to Consider the Ethical Implications of Emerging Technologies in the Breeding of Farm Animals.* Ministry of Agriculture, Fisheries and Food, HMSO: London.
- Frankena, W.K. (1973). *Ethics (Second Edition).* Englewood Cliffs, New Jersey: Prentice-Hall.
- Frankena, W.K. (1979). Ethics and the Environment, in K.E. Goodpaster & K.M. Sayre (Eds), *Ethics and Problems of the 21st Century.* Notre Dame/London: University Notre Dame Press.
- Grommers, F.J. (1997). Consciousness, science and conscience, in M. Dol, S. Kasanmoentalib, S. Lijmbach, E. Rivas, & R. van den Bos (Eds), *Animal Consciousness and Animal Ethics* (pp 198-207). Assen: Van Gorcum.
- Heeger, F.R. (1992). Eigenwert und Verantwortung. Zur normativen Argumentation in der Tierethiek, in W. Härle, M. Marquardt & W. Nethöfel (Eds), *Unsere Welt - Gottes Schöpfung* (pp 251-267). Marburg: Elwert Verlag.
- Holland, A. (1990). The Biotic Community: A Philosophical Critique of Genetic Engineering, in P. Wheale & R. McNally (Eds), *Animal Genetic Engineering: Of Pigs, Oncomice and Men.* London: Pluto Press.
- Lewis, C.I. (1946). *An Analysis of Knowledge and Valuation.* La Salle IL.
- Regan, T. (1984). *The Case for Animal Rights.* London: Routledge & Kegan Paul.
- Rutgers, L.J.E. (1993) *Het wel en wee der dieren: ethiek en diergeneeskundig handelen* (with a summary in English). PhD thesis Utrecht University.
- Rutgers, L.J.E., Grommers, F.J. & Colenbrander, B. (1996). Ethical Aspects of Invasive Reproduction Techniques in Farm Animals. *Reprod Dom Anim 31,* 651-655.
- Taylor, P.W. (1986). *Respect for Nature: A Theory of Environmental Ethics.* Princeton New Jersey: Princeton University Press.
- Von Wright, G.H. (1963). *The Varieties of Goodness.* London: Routledge.

4
Intrinsic value and species-specific behaviour[1]

Ruud van den Bos

In this paper the concepts of intrinsic value and species-specific behaviour are discussed and related to one another. It is argued that it is a (naturalistic) fallacy to attempt to define intrinsic value as a property of an individual animal based upon certain objective characteristics. Instead it is argued to define intrinsic value as a property of a relationship in terms of meaning or interest. Intrinsic value as opposed to instrumental value stresses the two-sidedness of the human-animal relationship: both are properties of this relationship. The concept of intrinsic value is important as buffer against unwarranted use of animals: animals may only be used when convincing reasons exist to do so, that is in order to fulfil e.g. our moral responsibilities towards our fellow humans. The concept aids in finding the balance between the moral principles and obligations inherent to the human-human ànd the human-animal relationship. Within the instrumental relationship several moral principles subsequently exist to safeguard the animals' interests: care for health, care for welfare, respect for integrity and respect for naturalness. These latter concepts belong to the moral as well as the biological domain with different referents being adequate in each domain. The concept of species-specific behaviour is common to these concepts in the biological domain. Depending upon the theoretical framework the concept of species-specific behaviour refers to a set of fixed patterns of behaviour or to a dynamic relationship between animal and environment of which control is an essential part. Only the latter concept has explanatory power. Whereas ethics sets the limits for the animals' living conditions (what we should do), biology shows whether, and if so how, this may be achieved given its theoretical frameworks (what we can do).

1. introduction

Since this book is about the concept of intrinsic value and since this chapter deals specifically with the relationship between the concepts of intrinsic value and species-specific behaviour I feel obliged to say more than just a few words on the concept of intrinsic value and to state how I conceive of the concept. Before doing so I would like to make some general comments on concepts.
Concepts refer to something, that is they have a specific referent (see Van den Bos & Kornet 1997). This referent may vary according to the theoretical framework within the specific domain in which the concept is used, be that a folk theory in common sense, a moral theory in ethics or a natural scientific theory in biology. A

concept can accordingly have more referents, even in one domain if competing theories exist in this domain. Once these different referents are defined a (rational) choice can be made for those referents which are *adequate* given the state of the art in each domain. Prescriptive definitions for each domain can then be given. This implies that these prescriptive definitions can differ between domains, accepting hereby the differences between domains. Adequacy should thus not be read as being synonymous to political or social desirability (see e.g. Van den Bos & Kornet 1997; Wiepkema 1995). Although this may seem to be but an academic point I will show what this amounts to when discussing the concepts of intrinsic value, animal welfare and species-specific behaviour.

2. intrinsic value: historic notes

The concept of intrinsic value has entered the ethical discussion to counteract the exclusive focus on the instrumental value that animals have in all kinds of economical and scientific activities (Verhoog 1992). The concept was meant to extend the circle of moral concern or the circle of entities having moral status from humans to animals and (even) beyond (see below), that is, to extend the circle of entities to which humans have to pay explicitly respect to or to explicitly justify their behaviour to.

For long moral reasoning with respect to animals was based on a Christian view in which humans have a God-given right to use animals (a view compatible with that of the Islam: Kruk 1997). Along with this right came the obligation to look after animals well, in other words to act as a good and justified steward. Good and justified refer hereby to being aware of the boundary between use and misuse, between exploitation and overexploitation. Accordingly this led to a 'Yes...provided that...' kind of ethics, which for long was part and parcel of Dutch society. The crumbling of the influence of Christianity in the Netherlands in the 1960's and 1970's and the intensifying of animal husbandry practices leading to the public awareness that the border to overexploitation of animals had been crossed has given room for new ideas. New concepts such as intrinsic value and animal welfare found their way in policies and ethical thinking in the 1980's. The God-given right to use animals was being questioned leading to (new) demands to justify the use and treatment of animals for human purposes - be that in the biomedical sciences or the agricultural sector - within a non-christian ethical framework (see below). This finally led to the completely opposite kind of 'No..unless...' kind of ethics: one has no right to use animals unless the purpose that they will be used for is of such importance that the 'No' may be violated (see below). The concept of intrinsic value serves as the basis of this 'No'.

3. intrinsic value: what does it mean?

The concept of intrinsic value is not an easy concept to understand or deal with. One reason is that it has been used in different ways in different contexts, that is in anthropocentric, zoocentric, biocentric and ecocentric ethical systems or combinations thereof (see Verhoog 1992 and Verhoog & Visser 1997 for an overview). This moving about of the concept seems partly the result of a continuous struggle to cover and keep up with the seemingly endless row of (apparent) moral problems generated by or counter-intuitive conclusions reached by new techniques, like transgenesis, or technical solutions to welfare problems, like selection or genetic manipulation of animals (see Verhoog 1992; Verhoog & Visser 1997).

One such a problematic point - nicely illustrated recently in an article in the Dutch newspaper *de Volkskrant* (Cornelissen 1997) - is whether intrinsic value should be conceived of as being independent of a human valuator per se. Or in other words, whether it is a *(natural) property of the individual animal.* Cornelissen (1997) not only concluded to a *contradictio in terminis* when the concept is defined such a way (it needs at least one human valuator to attribute intrinsic value to an animal; it is meaningless when there is no human left) but also subsequently ridiculed the concept on this ground by referring to cases in which mice (having intrinsic value as a natural property) put cats to trial for hunting and killing them (what gives cats the right to hunt and eat mice in such case).

Although one could argue in the latter case that cats behave according to their species-specific nature and accordingly should not be considered guilty (they can't help it) this will not solve the problem: for what is species-specific nature or behaviour? Is it that part of behaviour which is genetically determined and which is grounded in each and every individual? Cats spot a mouse and cannot help but hunt and kill it: is it a stimulus-response sequence built in through the process of natural selection in an endless row of ancestors? Is it that part of behaviour that is learned in immediate interaction with the environment, the result being more or less unique to each species? In other words, cats can also learn *not* to hunt mice? Indeed as Kuo showed in the 1930's cats do not hunt and kill for instance rats when adult if raised with rats as kittens (see Fantino & Logan 1979: 299). If hunting is meant for obtaining food will presenting them food on a regular basis solve the problem in addition?

Now one could carry on and on in this case but the problem is less whether or not an valuator exists per se (all human knowledge or human values are human-dependent and constitute human (physical or non-physical) reality in this sense; cf. Von Uexküll's Umwelt (Von Uexküll & Kriszat 1934)), but more which aspects or characteristics of animals would count as being morally relevant or not to the extent that animals are included in the moral circle, whether we are creating unjustly external referents by searching for objective characteristics to base decisions upon, and what the actual bases of human ethical systems are from which bio-ethical systems are derived. It is here where the real problems in my view start and where the question of the valuator and responsibility comes in. For, how to decide objectively what is morally relevant or not, or in other words, whether morally relevant differences exist between humans and other natural entities which justify a difference in moral treatment (see also Verhoog 1992 for discussion).

As a basis for having intrinsic value (or as the basis of the moral status of animals) people have proposed such characteristics as 'consciousness', 'psychological complexity', 'sentience' and 'being alive' (see e.g. Rivas 1997; Singer 1975; Verhoog & Visser 1997). Figure 1 summarizes what this amounts to. Verhoog & Visser (1997) criticize the consciousness- and sentience-view as being guided too

◇ individuals (of a species) having a certain characteristic
◯ individuals (of a species) lacking a certain characteristic
⊘ individuals (of a species) with moral status

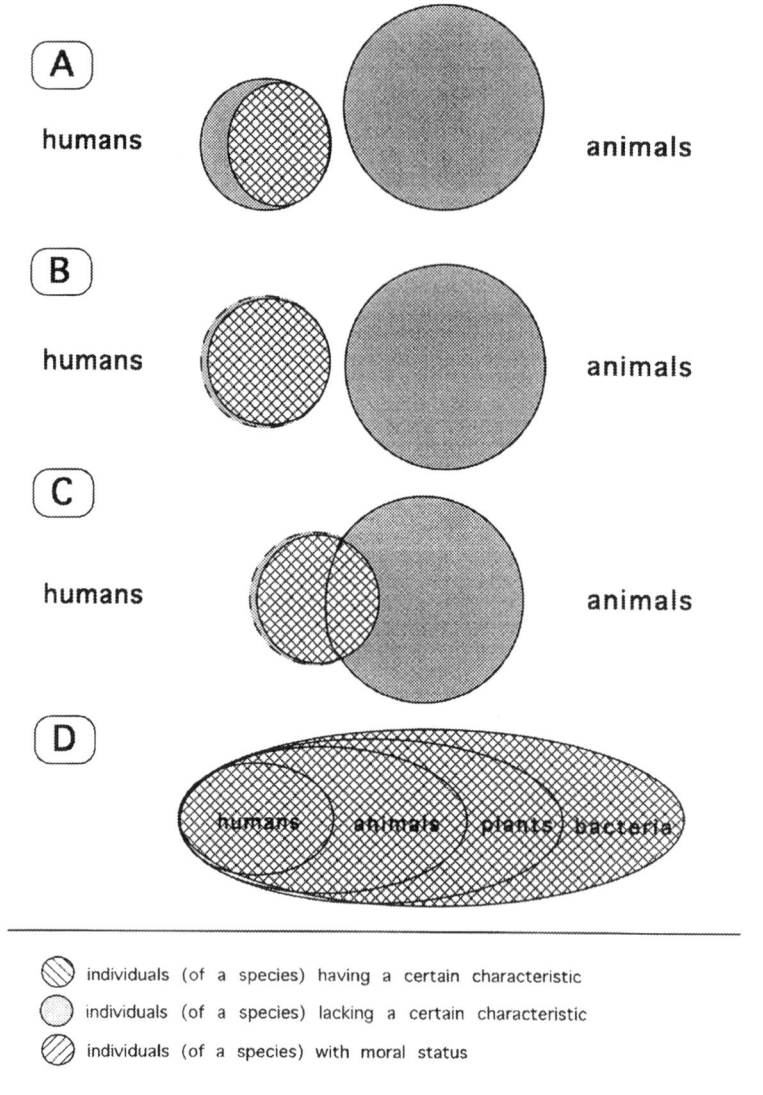

Figure 1: Diagrams to show the exclusion and inclusion of humans and animals based on specific objective characteristics, such as intelligence, psychological complexity, consciousness, sentience, capacity to suffer etc.

In panel A all animals are excluded since they lack the relevant characteristic (cf. Descartes, 1994 1637), some human individuals are excluded as well since they lack the relevant characteristic e.g. slaves, black people, women etc.; in panel B the latter is corrected for: all humans have intrinsic value (but see below); in panel C those species of animal are included which exhibit the relevant properties as well; in panel D being alive is the relevant characteristic leading to inclusion of all species of animal, plant and bacteria. It should be noted that in panel A, B and C, the boundaries between individuals (humans) or species (animals) which possess the relevant characteristic has a (somewhat) arbitrary character, which are inherent to the use of characteristics which are scalable. In humans (and animals as well actually) this also leads to the problem of marginal cases, such as severely mentally retarded people. In panels B and C they would still be excluded in principle (hence the dotted lines). In panel D logically not: they are all alive.

much by anthropocentric thinking (these aspects count as having a moral status for humans; figure 1a-c) and opt for more biocentric and ecocentric approaches with being alive a necessary condition to be awarded a moral status (intrinsic value of life; figure 1d) and the species-specific nature the sufficient condition to state what humans owe to various living creatures. They accordingly explicitly see a difference between plants, humans and animals in this sense. Rivas (1997) in contrast however goes so far as to consider flipping a coin the right, because unbiased, action in life-boat cases (e.g. three humans and a dog and one of them has to be set aboard to prevent the boat from sinking) in egalitarian systems based on consciousness and sentience in which he argues humans and animals logically have the same moral status (figure 1c). However, such a view puts a strong claim on how to determine whether, and if so which, animals are sentient or conscious. Although common sense would lead us to believe that animals are sentient and conscious, scientifically this is still debated (see Bermond 1996, 1997; Van den Bos 1996a,b). Furthermore even if so, the question arises whether all animals are conscious or whether differences would exist between say vertebrates and evertebrates (see Wiepkema 1985a,b, 1997). This would effectively mean that a kind of speciesism (such as 'family-ism', 'order-ism' etc.) which Rivas (1997) intends to fight may return at another level in the animal kingdom (compare figure 1c with figure 1d). I think that the Great Ape project in which apes are granted rights akin to human rights because of their human-like mental capacities and emotional life (Cavalieri & Singer 1993) is a prime example of this. Moreover, flipping a coin may according to humans be an unbiased action but not necessarily so according to animals. In fact, no animal is asked for its opinion in such cases. If for instance the life-boat would contain two humans, an aged dog and a puppy dog, it is not at all clear that flipping a coin would in the aged dog's view be the appropriate action. Since we cannot ask the dog's opinion it remains a human enterprise with sham objectivity.

In whatever way one views this search for an objective basis of intrinsic value to include animals in the moral circle I think that this search - extending in one way or another from the supposed basis of human morality, or referring to our place in nature as being one species among others - is as fruitless as the opposite way of referring to a God-given right to use animals. In both cases external referents are introduced and/or created to argue for or against the use of animals with the risk of running into closed, static, dogmatic ('Thou shallst not..') moral systems (see e.g. Philipse 1995).

In my view the essence of morality is the continuous and ongoing process of interpersonal justification of our behaviour and attitude towards other humans and towards our environment (see also de Cock Buning 1997). If there is no natural (God-given) right to use animals nor a natural right not to, but only a set of human conventions, which may serve as temporary basis, that is justifications cannot be based upon whatever objective or external referents without leading to fallacies of one kind or another, we have to recognize that we ourselves are the referents to base morality upon. This is the burden which humans carry and the dilemma which humans have to face: to find the balance between the responsibility towards humans (human-human ethical systems) and towards animals (human-animal ethical systems). In other words, intrinsic value cannot be viewed but in an anthropocentric view; not in the sense that humans are the absolute measure of everything, but in the sense that any moral principle, rule, obligation or concept is meant to say something about our *human* relationship with an entity, for which we have to justify our behaviour towards one another as *humans*. To include animals in the human moral domain can only be from the point of view of being human with a human view of morality: after all we are only human through, and in interaction with, other humans. This two-sidedness of the interaction with humans also determines human morality. Either stressing that humans are superior to animals referring to religious documents, or stressing that humans are similar to animals or just one species among other species, is not very helpful in this sense, and indeed is a running away from the responsibility to find the balance between our intellectual power to recreate the environment (in the broadest sense) to our own insights and the responsibilities which we have to our fellow humans and animals.

Personally I think therefore that the concept of intrinsic value should be defined merely (and is defined and used so by others as well; Van Hoogstraten 1997) as opposed to and in direct relationship with the concept of instrumental value such that the concepts are defined in each others context. In other words, intrinsic value is a value regardless of the *meaning* to or the *interest* that humans have in animals; instrumental value is the value which expresses this meaning or interest (see e.g. Van Hoogstraten 1997). In other words, intrinsic and instrumental value are *properties of the human-animal relationship* or indeed, when applied in a broader sense, *properties of relationships per se*. Moreover they are properties of a relationship which we may consider to be delicate because of the vulnerability of the parties involved, i.e. that we have to safeguard ourselves and others against misuse of these parties. In this context the concept of speciesism is of no value, for human morality in my view is equally not based on one objective capacity or the other (suffering, being alive etc.), but rather based on the need to safeguard ourselves against ourselves or as de Cock Buning (1997) argues to have control over our living conditions. In this view, these *objective* characteristics only come into play when instrumental relationships emerge (see below).

Rather than attributing an objective value to an individual animal the concept of intrinsic value therefore stresses the two-sidedness of the relationship between humans and animals: the instrumental and non-instrumental side. It says nothing about the relationship between animals or between species themselves, but everything, referring back to cats and mice, about the relationship between humans and cats, ànd the relationship between humans and mice.

Taking intrinsic value as moral principle does not imply therefore that animals may not be used at all, say for human purposes, i.e. that is to enter an instrumental relationship. For instance, we have a moral obligation towards fellow human beings to safeguard them from disease and to help them when diseased. Animals may contribute to meet this end in biomedical experiments. In other words, a clash in this case exists between humans and animals. In other words, the concept of intrinsic value forces us (i) to consider whether the proposed benefit to mankind justifies the use of animals and whether alternatives exist, and if not (ii) to do one's utmost best to safeguard the animal's perspective and interests once it is decided that it will be used for one means or another, i.e. that an instrumental relationship emerges. The first point will not be discussed in this chapter; the focus will be rather on the second.

4. instrumental value

```
┌─────────────────────────────────────────────────────────────────┐
│ moral domain                                                    │
│ (principles)                                                    │
│                        INTRINSIC  VALUE                         │
│                ─────────────────────────────────                │
│                       INSTRUMENTAL  VALUE                       │
│                                                                 │
│   ( care for )  ( care for )  ( respect for )  ( respect for )  │
│   (  health  )  ( welfare  )  (  integrity  )  (    nature   )  │
└─────────────────────────────────────────────────────────────────┘

┌─────────────────────────────────────────────────────────────────┐
│                                                                 │
│    ( health )    ( welfare )    ( integrity )    ( nature )     │
│                                                                 │
│              ( species - specific behaviour )                   │
│                                                                 │
│ biological domain                                               │
│     (states)                                                    │
└─────────────────────────────────────────────────────────────────┘
```

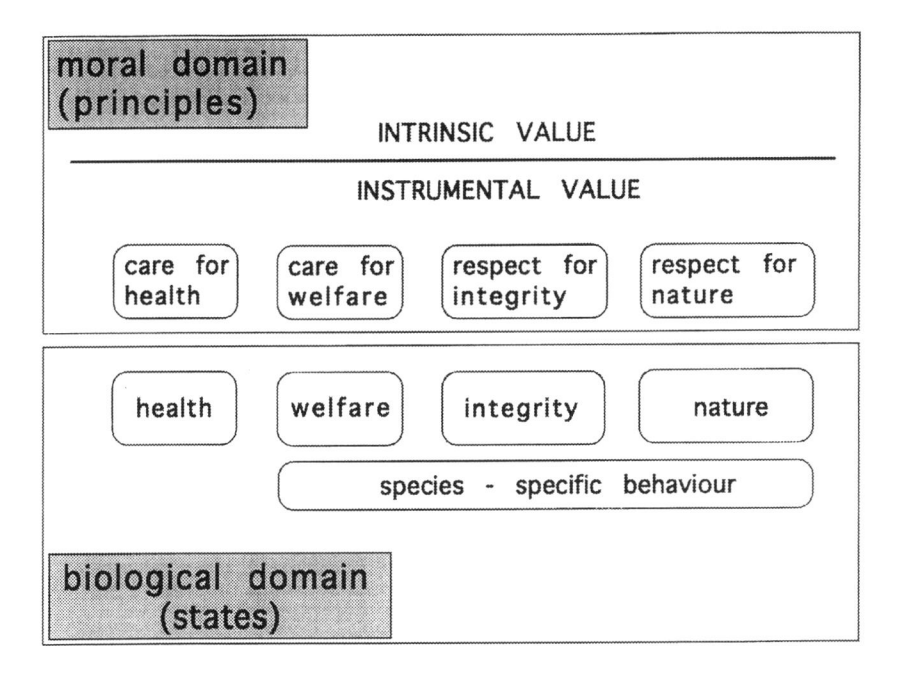

Figure 2: Relationship between concepts of the moral domain and the biological domain.

Figure 2 (Van den Bos & Kornet 1997) shows the various moral principles which come into play when an instrumental relationship emerges: care for health, care for welfare, respect for integrity and respect for naturalness. As figure 2 also shows the concepts of health, welfare, integrity and naturalness belong to two domains, that is to the moral ànd the biological domain.

As mentioned before it is important to stress that the meaning of these concepts in these different domains may differ. In other words, these domains should not be mixed since this leads to a confusion about what is adequate in each domain. I will illustrate this with the concept of animal welfare.

In common sense parlance the concept of animal welfare is cast into a concept of animal suffering or in general into a concept of animal feelings (experiences; see Van den Bos 1996a,b, 1997a; Dawkins 1980, 1990; Stafleu et al. 1996, 1997; Wemelsfelder 1993, 1997). In the moral domain such a use of the concept easily fits in with moral thinking since it can be tied to the moral principle of promoting good or avoiding harm: to promote animal welfare, that is to promote that animals feel good (approaching welfare from the positive side) or do not suffer (approaching welfare from the negative side). However, in contrast such a use of the concept of animal welfare does not easily fit in with current thinking in the biological domain conceived of in the natural sciences's sense. Historically neither ethology nor comparative psychology (adopting the natural sciences's methodology) have given room to feelings or the like (as can be read for instance in Tinbergen's 1951 classic *The study of Instinct*; see e.g. Baerends 1978; Van den Bos 1996a,b, 1997a,b; Vossen 1996; Wemelsfelder 1993, 1995, 1996, 1997). Within this framework welfare is cast in terms of successful adaptation to particular (artificial) environments (Broom & Johnson 1995) which in practice is approached from the negative side using long-term stress symptoms as indicators of failure to adapt and hence of a state of 'non-welfare' (see Baerends 1978; Wiepkema 1985a,b, 1996). As Stafleu et al. (1996, 1997) note this use, however adequate in the biological domain, has no direct relationship to principles in the moral domain. This is turn has led to tension between moral and biological thinking with some people stressing that welfare has to do with feelings and nothing else, which in other words should be the basis, or at least the guiding principle, of biological thinking as well (e.g. Dawkins 1980, 1990; Wemelsfelder 1997).

One strategy which has been employed to overcome this seemingly wide gap is to call analogous reasoning to help. This reasoning states that given the similarity in responses of humans and animals in situations which humans experience as pleasant or unpleasant, and the similarity of the way the central nervous systems of humans and animals is organized, it is likely or plausible (and no more than that) that animals will have such experiences as well (see Stafleu et al. 1992; this postulate stems originally from Romanes who intended to complete Darwin's programme on the continuity between animals and humans in the psychological domain). The methodology of ethology and comparative psychology (analysing patterns of behaviour in relation to stimuli and physiology) combined with the postulate will lead then to a concept of welfare, in which feelings indirectly play a role.

To treat animals if they have experiences through analogous reasoning as a principle of 'Benefit of the Doubt' can be justified by stating that less harm will be done using this principle than by not using it should it finally turn out that animals have experiences. However sympathetic for the purpose of filling in and saving the feelings-part of the concept of animal welfare, the analogy postulate is a weak scientific position of which the premises on further inspection are so weak that one must conclude that the similarity of feelings outcome has no meaning whatsoever (see Bermond 1997; Van den Bos 1997a). Although I will not elaborate any further on this matter here (see Van den Bos 1997a for arguments against the analogy postulate; see also Bermond 1997) it should be noted that the fact that ethology and comparative psychology left feelings out of their research field is based on a specific philosophical view of human feelings embedded in the Cartesian (Descartes 1994/1637) capacity of introspection of, or the capacity of discrimination or reflection of, the independent ghostly 'I' which is opposed to the physical body (Tinbergen 1951; Bermond 1996, 1997). This non-physical 'I' escapes natural sciences, which only deals (directly or indirectly) with physical reality. It is not the proper place here to elaborate on the ways how for instance Wemelsfelder (1993, 1996, 1997) and Van den Bos (1997a,b) have each dealt with this problem leading to two entirely different outcomes and outlooks on the problem at hand. It suffices to say that Wemelsfelder takes a non-reductionistic, common sense embedded, realist view on the matter of feelings (or consciousness in general), whereas Van den Bos takes a reductionistic, neurobiology embedded, instrumentalist view on this same matter. Wemelsfelder's view is formally not cast into natural sciences, whereas Van den Bos's view is. Wemelsfelder's view on welfare is immediately cast in terms of feelings, Van den Bos's view only indirectly.

No matter how one views the problem it is clear that the referent which is adequate in one domain is not necessarily so in another. The relationship in this sense between ethics or ethics based on common sense, with its principles of what we should do, and natural sciences with its principles what we can say directly and indirectly about physical reality is a tense one. As the discussion of animal welfare shows, three things might actually happen (see figure 3). First, within natural sciences, i.c. ethology and comparative psychology as natural sciences, a common

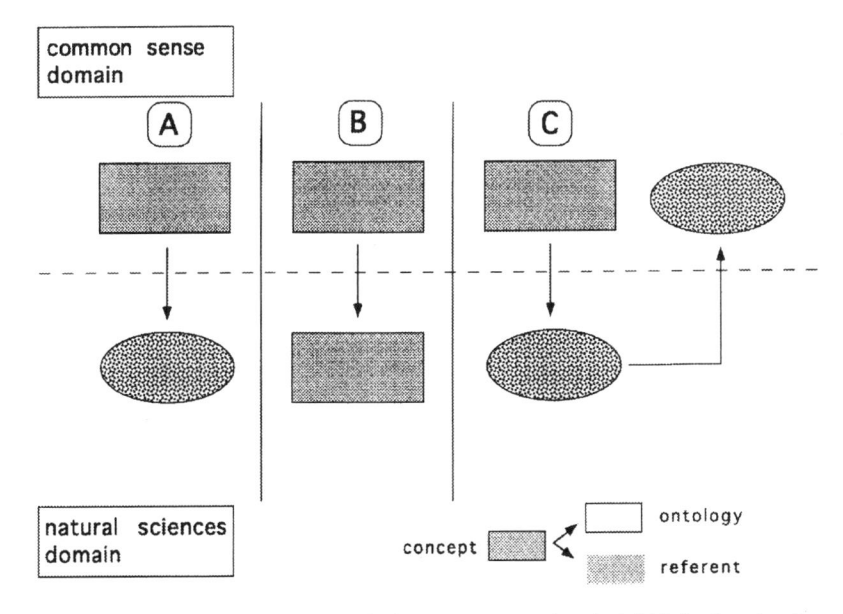

Figure 3: Relationship between concepts in the common sense domain (which for the sake of argument is directly seen as the moral domain (ethics)) and the biological domain (natural sciences). In panel A natural sciences changes the contents of concept to the extent that it is different from the original common sense concept; in panel B natural sciences starts with the common sense concept; in panel C natural sciences not only changes the contents of the concept to the extent that it fits its domain but also changes its ontological status such that the original common sense concept may disappear as being inadequate. An example of the latter is the change of the original medieval common sense view that the earth is our solar system's centre to the scientifically changed new common sense view that the sun is our solar system's centre.

sense concept is redefined within natural sciences's current theoretical frameworks and current methodology without questioning or analysing the (implicit) presuppositions and ontological status of (i) the common sense concept itself, and (ii) of current scientific reasons why the common sense concept does not fit natural sciences's frameworks and methodology (cf. Baerends 1978). Although scientifically adequate, the scientific concept has little or no moral bearing or common sense ground left. Furthermore, the challenge posed by the common sense concept has been left for the safety of current scientific thinking. Second, common sense concepts (or moral concepts) are the starting point of study and the natural sciences's methodology is adequate or applies in so far it goes (cf. Wemelsfelder 1993). Although with direct moral bearing and - logically - common sense understanding, the scientific status of this enterprise is weak. Third, within natural sciences the common sense (or moral) concept is not simply redefined to fit its current limits, but rather the implicit presuppositions and ontological status of the common sense concept and of current scientific thinking about the common sense concept are exposed such that new routes of scientific thinking about and empirical studies of the concept are opened with the effect that the common sense concept may change as well in the long run (leading to evolution of common sense concepts; cf. Van den Bos 1997a; Smith Churchland 1986). Although scientifically adequate it poses a threat to common sense and morality (see Dennett 1991: 448). Thus various benefits and costs are attached to these relationships between using and/or analysing concepts in the common sense and natural scientific domain. In any event however, if desirability and adequacy are mixed - no matter how noble the case one argues for - this not only erodes the status of the domains but also the quest for understanding the matter in each domain separately (see also Wiepkema 1995). Furthermore it leads to confusion about the relationship between and the status of common sense, ethics based hereon and natural sciences. It is not my aim to discuss the concepts of health, integrity and naturalness here, for this is done in other chapters of this book (integrity (chapter by Rutgers); naturalness: (chapter by Visser & Verhoog)). What I would like to do in the remaining part is to analyze the concept of species-specific behaviour in the biological domain. This concept is common to the concept of animal welfare (if animals are able to behave according to their species-specific behaviour or needs than their welfare is supposed to be promoted), integrity (which refers to autonomy, wholeness and species-specificity (Rutgers, this book; Grommers et al. 1995)) and naturalness (which refers to species-specific being (Visser & Verhoog, this book)). This concept is often used in the context of creating appropriate housing conditions. For instance, in Dutch legislation it is stated that housing facilities should contain elements such that animals can show species-specific behaviour (Animal Health and Welfare Act).

5. species-specific behaviour

5.1. introduction

The words species-specific behaviour suggest that *behaviour* exists which is *specific* (or *unique* or *characteristic*) for a particular *species*, such that species A and B can be differentiated along the presence of this or that behaviour. This implies that all individuals of the species should show the same behaviour as well, for which subsequently a genetic basis in one way or another may be supposed. Accordingly individual variation in behaviours would not qualify as species-specific behaviour, but rather as individual-specific or idiosyncratic behaviour. The latter may be due to the peculiar circumstances under which the individuals are held. In any event, a genetic basis is not supposed for such behaviour. Furthermore any behaviour which individuals of different species share is not species-specific in this sense as well, but is rather for instance genus-specific, family-specific and so on. In this way behaviour can be used for taxonomy and phylogenetic reconstruction.

5.2. species-specific behaviour as fixed action patterns
This concept of species-specific behaviour emerged in the early ethological tradition of Lorenz and Tinbergen and refers to *(a class of) fixed genetically anchored behavioural patterns which emerge in (and actually even independently from) a specific environment* as the result of the activation of motivational systems which are crucial to the survival of the individual (biologically relevant systems) such as the sexual, hunger, thirst motivational systems (see textbooks by Alcock 1975; Barnard 1983; Fantino & Logan 1979; Gould 1982; Hall 1983; Huntingford 1984; Manning 1979; Manning & Stamp Dawkins 1992; McFarland 1993; Stamp Dawkins 1986). In fact these patterns are also know as fixed-action patterns, innate behaviours or consummatory behaviours. They are considered to be the end-products of a system set in motion by changes in physiological variables and external stimuli (sign-stimuli), and cast in motivationally oriented behavioural models. Appetitive behavioural patterns in this context refer to that part of behaviour which precedes the consummatory behavioural patterns, and exposes the exploratory or searching part of behaviour. The different ecological factors under which the different (individuals of) species live have shaped or determined through the process of natural selection in a long row of ancestors the differences of these end-products between species. *Species-specific behaviour* therefore refers to *a set of genetically fixed behavioural patterns unique for a species.*

For long species-specific behavioural patterns were in the centre of the nature-nurture discussion: they referred to a class of patterns which emerged in (and even so independently from) a specific environment, genetically fixed and genetically determined, and tied to the activation of systems crucial for survival (see above mentioned textbooks). Or as Lorenz used as metaphor: genes as the blueprint of a building for which the environment delivers the right materials to construct the building (McFarland 1993:29). These patterns stood in sharp contrast to the learned behavioural patterns (or strategies) like those seen in e.g. Skinner-boxes in which behavioural patterns (or strategies) were shaped through interaction of aspects of the external environment and internal reward-related processes. As such it referred directly to the difference between ethology (which studied fixed action patterns in the field) and comparative psychology (which studied the learned patterns in the laboratory). This distinction has been resolved as being an inadequate way of looking at behavioural patterns, as if they belong to two different and opposing ontological classes of behaviour. For instance, the broken wing display of plovers to lure predators away from the nests emerges in all nesting plovers (species-specific behavioural patterns in this sense), but how to maximize and adjust the effect of this display to the circumstances is learned in interaction with various predators. Furthermore, it was abundantly demonstrated that also learning abilities have a genetic basis.

5.3. behaviour as a process

The blue-print view has been replaced by the view that the expression of all behavioural patterns is the resultant of the interaction of genes with the environment (taken in its broadest sense; see below) in the developing organism, or in other words: behavioural patterns (or sequences thereof) are the result of the interaction of genotype, phenotype and environment, or emerge by a process called 'epigenesis, by which each developmental event sets the stage for, but does not dictate the next' (McFarland 1993: 29; figure 4). Thus the view that behavioural patterns are genetically determined in the sense that gene A codes for pattern A in a 1 to 1 relationship has been abandoned for a view in which differences between the presence of genes may result in differences between patterns. To be more precise: differences between patterns may be the result of differences in genotype (if all other factors are the same; genes do not code for behavioural patterns but differences between individuals regarding behavioural patterns may be due to differences in (the presence of) genes (no matter how narrowly or broadly defined; Maynard Smith 1988)), differences in phenotype (the developmental history of the individual if all other factors are the same) or environment (the environmental stressors which impinge onto the developing organism if all other factors are the same) (figure 4). As an illustration what this amounts to the following discussion by McFarland (1993:30) nicely shows how the difference between learned or innate behaviour in altricial and precocial species vanishes if one takes a second look.

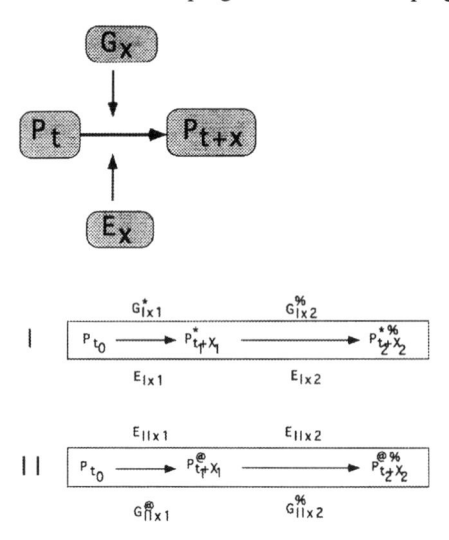

It is interesting to explore the relationship between learned and innate, or non-learned, behaviour by comparing the baby bird of a *precocial* species (a species in which hatching occurs late in development) to the baby of an *altricial* species (a species in which hatching

Figure 4: Interaction between genotype, phenotype and environment.
Phenotype at time t+x is dependent on the genes (G) active during time-interval x and the environment (E) present during this interval, and the phenotype at time t. Bars indicate how differences in phenotypes of 2 individuals (I,II) emerge due to e.g. a genetic difference in interval x1.

occurs early). If two such birds are compared at the same stage of physical development, such as the point at which the first feathers appear, we find that the precocial bird is still inside the egg, while the altricial bird has already hatched. By the time the precocial bird hatches, the altricial juvenile has had the opportunity to learn a great deal, while the precocial bird has not yet begun to learn. What we find interestingly, is that the precocial hatchling may have innately developed capabilities which the altricial chick has had to learn. For example, the altricial white-crowned sparrow learns the song of its species while a nestling. By contrast, chickens are precocial, passing early infancy while still in the egg, but they have the innate ability to produce normal vocalizations, even though never previously exposed to them.

We may be inclined to think of what happens inside the egg as being purely maturational, in the sense that the relevant environmental factors are predetermined. We should not forget, however, that the normal environment of the white-crowned sparrow also is predetermined in the sense that the nestlings normally hear the song of their own species during the critical period of song learning.

In other words, learned behaviour and innate behaviour are rather labels than explanatory concepts. They mask the common underlying mechanisms and suggest different developmental pathways whereas there are actually no basic differences. Moreover it shows that the idea of 'environment' as being only relevant from birth onwards is misleading: from the moment of conception onwards the idea of environment is relevant. It is only the stage of development which determines how extended or limited the idea of environment and relevant factors (whichever they are) therein should be taken.

Therefore, as far as the concept of species-specific behaviour is still used in ethology nowadays it refers to a class of patterns in a descriptional sense (a class of patterns which seems to emerge in all individuals of a given species regardless of the specific environment and of the developmental history) rather than in explanatory sense.

This dynamic picture leads automatically to the idea of behaviour as a process: the continuous interaction of the individual with its environment. Some of the products of this process have been laid down in all individuals of the species and emerge more or less the same in all of them (they are behavioural patterns which require highly stable (micro)environments to be selected across generations), others are more variable and emerge in interaction with the specific environment in which individuals learn to act in relationship to events (predict and control events in a more variable environment). In this sense the capacity to learn has been selected as a successful trait to act in a variable environment, not what should be specifically learned (the end-result).

5.4. species-specific behaviour in a control model

An example of a behavioural model which integrates (partly) these two elements using behaviour as a process is the negative feedback control model of Wiepkema (1985a,b). Behavioural programmes in this model are meant to reduce the mismatch between the actual input (Istwert) and a given reference value (Sollwert). This mismatch may occur at the physiological level (internal homeostasis: motivation with fixed behavioural programmes) or in interaction with the environment (external homeostasis: learning with more flexible programmes): behaviour is the reaction to this mismatch. The model stresses the elements of predictability and controllability as important aspects of the interaction with the environment. Furthermore the model contains emotions as functional signals to indicate whether programmes act in the right direction or not: negative emotions if the mismatch becomes larger, positive emotions of the mismatch becomes smaller. Within this model all individuals of a species possess the ability to predict and control changes in their environment, i.e. the ability to learn. Differences of course may emerge between individuals in the extent to which they are able to use this ability. In each species control is maximal to the extent it is needed to survive in its niche. In other words, differences between species may arise in the extent to which this capacity to predict and control applies is extended and needed (Wiepkema 1997).

Within this model *species-specific behaviour* therefore refers to *species-specific interaction with the environment with behavioural programmes which are either fixed or flexible* or in short *species-specific control to maintain homeostasis*.

Although this model integrates both aspects of behaviour, lacking from this model is the developmental side of individuals. The expression of genes and the effects of the environment always take place within a developing phenotype. Both the motivational models and this Wiepkema-model have a strong emphasis on the adult-phase of interaction of the organism with its environment. Very little attention is paid to how the organism develops into the adult-stage. Furthermore neither the motivational models nor the Wiepkema model link brain and behaviour, and leave consciousness out of the picture. I previously (1997a) discussed a model that incorporates these aspects as well.

5.5. behaviour as process of the nervous system

I will not elaborate extensively on this model here since I have done this elsewhere (Van den Bos 1997a) but just mention a few important points (see also above): the model is a hierarchical negative feedback model of the organisation of the brain in which behaviour is the control of input. Behaviour is goal-maintenance in a dynamic neural system. Behaviour (transitions of brain or neural states) is expressed as transitions of arbitrarily labelled behavioural patterns and transitions of arbitrarily labelled mental states (which I define as consciousness). Ultimately mental states can be reduced onto brain (neural) states. Those patterns which emerge regardless of the environment are selected as part of (dedicated) neural networks which recognize, process information and respond in 'programmed' ways. The capacity to learn is also selected as network per se in which actual input and output determine what is learned. It is important to state that environment in this model formally refers to everything outside the nervous system, or in other words all environmental events have an effect on developing neural networks, which determine behavioural patterns and mental states. Within this context the concept of *species-specific behaviour* refers to *species-specific dynamic neural network activity expressed as behavioural patterns and mental states* or in short *species-specific dynamic control of input*.

5.6. species-specific behaviour

The concept of species-specific behaviour has accordingly different referents depending on the specific model and theoretical framework it is used in. It may be conceived of as referring to statically labelled patterns of behaviour per se or as a *dynamic interaction* of the organism with its environment in which behavioural patterns and behavioural capacities are both important components and of which control is the crucial element (de Cock Buning's notion of control; de Cock Buning

1997). Only the latter concept has explanatory power. It should be noted that these different referents have different consequences when being applied to create suitable housing conditions (Van den Bos, in preparation).

6. Conclusion

Human morality, or the set of human moral rules, may be viewed in the context of regulating human behaviour and attitude towards the environment in its broadest sense (be that conspecifics, plant or animal species, ecosystems etc.). As de Cock Buning (1997) argued morality may be viewed as the outcome of the urge to have control over one's situation. Absolute foundations with respect to the moral status of animals captured in an objectively based concept of intrinsic value may lead to closed, static and dogmatic moral systems (Philipse 1995). Rather, defining and using intrinsic value in relationship with instrumental value may lead to open and dynamic moral systems. Indeed, as Philipse (1995) argued presently existing moral systems may be replaced by others in the future if they are better adapted to or meet new and changed circumstances through a process akin to natural selection. Accordingly the contents of these moral rules may vary according to the specific circumstances while the urge to have moral rules per se remains. The concept of intrinsic value along with that of instrumental value forces us to balance our moral obligations towards our fellow human beings and animals all the time. This balance may shift over time according to changing circumstances and needs. Whereas ethics sets the limits for the animals' living conditions (what we should do), biology shows whether, and if so how, this may be achieved given its theoretical frameworks (what we can do). De Cock Buning (1997) formulated as moral universal that one ought to guarantee each animal which crosses our path full control over its situation from its own species-specific perspective. This moral universal is a practical common denominator of the care for welfare, respect for integrity and respect for naturalness. How to guarantee this is then a matter of understanding in the biological domain what the determinants are of how animals exert control over their situation in their natural habitat, such that this can also be guaranteed in an artificial environment. This refers directly to the models of Wiepkema (1985a,b) and Van den Bos (1997a).

Note

[1] This paper was written with help of a grant of the research programme 'Ethics and Policies' which is subsidized by the Netherlands Research Organization (NWO) and the Ministries of (i) Agriculture, Nature Management and Fisheries (LNV), (ii) Health, Welfare and Sports (VWS) and (iii) Education, Culture and Science (OC&W).

Literature

- Alcock, J. (1975). *Animal behaviour: an evolutionary approach*. Sunderland MA: Sinauer Associates Inc.
- Baerends, G. P. (1978). Welzijn: vanuit de ethologie bezien (Welfare as seen from an ethological point of view), in J.J. Groen en A.D. de Groot (Eds.) *Over welzijn: Criterium, Onderzoeksobject, Beleidsdoel* (*On welfare: Criterion, Research subject, Policy goal*) (pp.83-106). Deventer: Van Loghum Slaterus.
- Barnard, C.J. (1983). *Animal behaviour, ecology and evolution*. London: Helm
- Bermond, B. (1996). Dierenleed: een neuropsychologische analyse van moedwil en misverstand (Animal suffering: a neuropsychological analysis of malice and misunderstanding). *Nederlands Tijdschrift voor de Psychologie, 51*, 121-134.
- Bermond, B. (1997). The myth of animal suffering, in M. Dol, S. Kasanmoentalib, S. Lijmbach, E. Rivas en R. van den Bos (Eds.) *Animal consciousness and Animal ethics; Perspectives from the Netherlands* (pp. 125-143) Assen: Van Gorcum. *Animals in Philosophy and Science vol.1*.
- Bos, van den R. (1996a). Wetenschap en Welzijn: de kleren van de keizer? (Science and Welfare: the emperor's clothes?), in R. van den Bos (Ed.) *Welzijn van dieren en wetenschap: Door welke bril kijkt u?* (*Animal Welfare and Science: Which pair of glasses are you wearing?*) (pp. 1-6). Tilburg: Tilburg University Press.
- Bos, van den R. (1996b). Welzijn van dieren en Wetenschap (Animal Welfare and Science). *NVG-mededelingenblad, 5(1)*, 10-21.
- Bos, van den R. (1997a). Reflections on the organisation of mind, brain and behaviour, in M. Dol, S. Kasanmoentalib, S. Lijmbach, E. Rivas en R. van den Bos (Eds.) *Animal consciousness and Animal ethics; Perspectives from the Netherlands* (pp. 144-166). Assen: Van Gorcum, *Animals in Philosophy and Science vol.1*.
- Bos, van den R. (1997b). Welzijn van dieren en dierenwelzijnsbeleid: een kritische inleiding (Animal welfare and animal welfare policies: a critical introduction), in R. van den Bos (Ed.) *Welzijn van dieren en dierenwelzijnsbeleid* (*Animal Welfare and Animal Welfare Policies*) (pp. 1-18). Tilburg: Tilburg University Press.
- Bos, van den R. & Kornet, D.J. (1997) Ethiek en Beleid: Samenhang der Begrippen (Ethics and Policies: Connecting concepts); Expertseminar Dier- en Natuurethiek, Stimuleringsprogramma *Ethiek en Beleid* 6 december 1996 (In: Jaarverslag Geesteswetenschappen, NWO, (pp. 101-103), Year report Humanities, Netherlands Research Organization, pp. 101-103).
- Broom, D.M. & Johnson, K.G. (1993). *Stress and animal welfare*. London: Chapman & Hall
- Cavalieri, P. & Singer, P. (1993). *The Great Ape Project: Equality beyond Humanity*. London: fourth Estate
- Cock Buning, de Tj. (1997). Animal ethics or the conscious control of the *Umwelt*, in M. Dol, S. Kasanmoentalib, S. Lijmbach, E. Rivas en R. van den Bos (Eds.) *Animal consciousness and Animal ethics; Perspectives from the Netherlands* (pp. 185-197). Assen: Van Gorcum, *Animals in Philosophy and Science vol.1*.
- Cornelissen, A. (1997). Waarde van dier is alleen door de mens te bepalen (The animal's value is only to be determined by humans). *Volkskrant 27 januari 1997*, 7.
- Dawkins, M.S. (1980). *Animal suffering. The science of animal welfare*. London: Chapman & Hall.
- Dawkins, M.S. (1986). *Unravelling animal behaviour*. Harlow: Longman Group Ltd.
- Dawkins, M.S. (1990). From an animal's point of view: Motivation, fitness, and animal welfare, *Behavioural and Brain Sciences, 13*, 1-61
- Dennett, D.C. (1991). *Consciousness explained*. London: Penguin books.
- Descartes, R. (1994). *Over de methode* (*Discourse de la Methode*). Meppel: Boom Klassiek (original work published in 1637).
- Fantino, E. & Logan, C.A. (1979). *The experimental analysis of behaviour: A biological approach*. San Francisco: W.H. Freeman & Co.
- Gould, J.L. (1982). *Ethology: the mechanism and evolution of behavior*. New York & London: W.W. Norton & Co.
- Grommers, F.J., Rutgers, L.J.E, & Wijsmuller, J.M. (1995). Welzijn - Intrinsieke waarde - Integriteit (Welfare - Intrinsic Value - Integrity). *Tijdschrift voor Diergeneeskunde, 120*, 490-494.
- Hall, G. (1983). *Behaviour. An introduction to psychology as a biological science*. London: Academic Press

- Hoogstraten, van S. (1997) Welzijn van dieren en dierenwelzijnsbeleid: Doelstellingen van het Ministerie van Volksgezindheid, Welzijn en Sport (Animal welfare and animal welfare policies: policy goals of the Ministry of Health, Welfare and Sports). In R. van den Bos (Ed.) *Welzijn van dieren en dierenwelzijnsbeleid (Animal Welfare and Animal Welfare Policies)* (pp. 23-29). Tilburg: Tilburg University Press.
- Huntingford, F. (1984). *The study of animal behaviour.* London: Chapman & Hall.
- Kruk, R. (1997) Islamische visies op de rechten van het dier (Islamic views on animal rights), in R. van den Bos (Ed.) *Welzijn van dieren en dierenwelzijnsbeleid (Animal Welfare and Animal Welfare Policies)* (pp. 83-97). Tilburg: Tilburg University Press.
- Manning, A. (1979). *An introduction to animal behaviour.* 3rd ed. London: Edward Arnold (Publishers) Ltd.
- Manning, A. & Dawkins, M.S. (1992). *An introduction to animal behaviour.* 4th edition, Cambridge: Cambridge University Press.
- Maynard Smith, J.W. (1988). *Did Darwin get it right?* London: Penguin Books
- McFarland, D. (1993) *Animal behaviour; Psychobiology, ethology and evolution.* 2nd ed. Harlow (Essex): Addison Wesley Longman Ltd.
- Philipse, H. (1995). *Atheistisch manifest; Drie wijsgerige opstellen over godsdienst en moraal (Atheistic manifest; Three philosophical essays on religion and morality).* Amsterdam: Prometheus
- Rivas, E. (1997). Psychological complexity and animal ethics: choosing between hierarchy and equality, in M. Dol, S. Kasanmoentalib, S. Lijmbach, E. Rivas en R. van den Bos (Eds.) *Animal consciousness and Animal ethics; Perspectives from the Netherlands* (pp. 169-184) Assen: Van Gorcum. Animals in Philosophy and Science vol.1.
- Singer, P. (1975). *Animal Liberation.* New York: Avon Books.
- Smith Churchland, P. (1986). *Neurophilosophy; Toward a unified science of the mind/brain.* Cambridge (MA): A Bradford Book, The MIT Press.
- Stafleu, F.R., Rivas, E., Rivas T., Vorstenbosch, J., Heeger, F.R. & Beynen, A.C. (1992). The use of analogous reasoning for assessing discomfort in laboratory animals. *Animal Welfare, 1,* 77-84.
- Stafleu, F.R., Grommers, F.J. & Vorstenbosch, J. (1996). Animal welfare: evolution and erosion of a moral concept. *Animal Welfare, 5,* 225-234.
- Stafleu, F.R., Grommers, F.J. & Vorstenbosch, J. (1997). Animal welfare: a hierarchy of concepts. (unpublished manuscript).
- Tinbergen, N. (1951). *The Study of Instinct.* Oxford: Clarendon Press.
- Verhoog. H. (1992) The concept of intrinsic value and transgenic animals. *Journal of Agricultural and Environmental Ethics, 5,* 147-160
- Verhoog, H. & Visser, T. (1997). A view of intrinsic value not based on animal consciousness, in M. Dol, S. Kasanmoentalib, S. Lijmbach, E. Rivas en R. van den Bos (Eds.) *Animal consciousness and Animal ethics; Perspectives from the Netherlands* (pp. 223-232) Assen: Van Gorcum. Animals in Philosophy and Science vol.1.
- Von Uexküll, J., & Kriszat G. (1934). *Streifzuege durch die Umwelten von Tieren und Menschen (Strolls through the environments of animals and humans).* Berlin: Verlag von Julius Springer.
- Vossen, J. (1996). Ethologie, psychologie en welzijn? (Ethology, psychology and welfare?), in R. van den Bos (Ed.) *Welzijn van dieren en wetenschap: Door welke bril kijkt u? (Animal Welfare and Science: Which pair of glasses are you wearing?)* (pp. 39-46). Tilburg: Tilburg University Press.
- Wemelsfelder, F. (1993). *Animal Boredom: Towards an empirical approach of subjectivity.* Proefschrift RUL.
- Wemelsfelder, F. (1995). Dierlijke subjectiviteit: een meetbaar begrip? (Animal subjectivity: a measurable concept?). *NVG mededelingenblad, 4.*
- Wemelsfelder, F. (1996). Het meten van welzijn bij dieren (Measuring animal welfare), in R. van den Bos (Ed.). *Welzijn van dieren en wetenschap: Door welke bril kijkt u? (Animal Welfare and Science: Which pair of glasses are you wearing?)* (pp. 55-62). Tilburg: Tilburg University Press.
- Wemelsfelder, F. (1997). Investigating the animal's point of view. An enquiry into a subject-based method of measurement in the field of animal welfare, in M. Dol, S. Kasanmoentalib, S. Lijmbach, E. Rivas en R. van den Bos (Eds.) *Animal consciousness and Animal ethics; Perspectives from the Netherlands* (pp. 73-89) Assen: Van Gorcum. Animals in Philosophy and Science vol.1.
- Wiepkema, P. (1985a). Over gedragsstoringen bij dieren in de veehouderij (On behavioural problems in animal farming). *Tijdschrift voor Diergeneeskunde, 110,* 12-20.
- Wiepkema, P. (1985b). Abnormal behaviours in farm animals: ethological implications. *The Netherlands Journal of Zoology, 35,* 279-299.

- Wiepkema, P. (1995). Deugdelijk of welgevallig: dat is de kwestie (Adequate or desirable: that's the issue) (unpublished manuscript 7-2-1995)
- Wiepkema, P. (1996). Besef en beleving bij dieren (Animal consciousness and animal awareness), in R. van den Bos (Ed.) *Welzijn van dieren en wetenschap: Door welke bril kijkt u?* (*Animal Welfare and Science: Which pair of glasses are you wearing?*) (pp. 23-30). Tilburg: Tilburg University Press.
- Wiepkema, P. (1997). The emotional vertebrate, in M. Dol, S. Kasanmoentalib, S. Lijmbach, E. Rivas en R. van den Bos (Eds.) *Animal consciousness and Animal ethics; Perspectives from the Netherlands* (pp. 93-102) Assen: Van Gorcum. *Animals in Philosophy and Science vol.1.*

Incompatibility of intrinsic value with genetic manipulation

Thijs Visser

Anyone who respects Nature for its own sake and who gives it due moral consideration will have no problem recognizing its intrinsic value. The question discussed in this paper is whether genetic manipulation (of animals[1]) is compatible with nature's intrinsic value. Proponents of genetic engineering use mainly two kind of arguments:
1. the naturalistic argument: genetic engineering is a natural proceeding, because it applies the same kind of mechanisms and processes nature does,
2. the historical argument: genetic engineering is another kind of technique mankind has applied for breeding animals for times immemorial, only quicker, more accurate, and efficient.

Both kinds of arguments I shall analyze critically and eventually reject from both an empirical and an ethical point of view. Finally I shall give a short overview of the Dutch policy regarding genetic engineering.

1. The naturalistic argument

In ethics the 'naturalistic fallacy' is a kind of error of moral argumentation in which moral values are derived from empirical facts, or in the customary English idiom: 'when an *'ought'* is derived from an *'is'*. This view on ethics is generally considered morally false, which has been argued over and over. Here it will be argued that in the case of genetic manipulation the argumentation is empirically and formally wrong as well.

In dispute and evaluation of human action nature or naturalness never can be used as an argument, neither as proof, nor as disproof. Concerning genetic manipulation: "...and the reference to nature is (...) when it applies to actions, no argument. Who manipulates genes, does *not* act like nature, but exactly while he does *act*, it is not the same."[2] (authors' translation)

It is obvious that 'nature' is not an unambiguous concept. Nearly every definition of 'nature' meets with countless exceptions, deviations, or even contradictions. That goes for the laws of nature as well. Even man's place in nature is dubious, like in the following citation: 'Is man a part of nature, or is man apart from nature?'. This eternal philosophical question will not be answered here, however.

1.1. Species Barriers
Leaving philosophy and ethics momentarily aside, I shall look first at the empirical

content of the naturalistic argument: whether genetic engineering applies the same kind of mechanisms and processes nature does. When 'biotechnique' means a technique used for manipulating living matter, it is rather absurd to assert that nature uses the same technique, *viz.* genetic engineering, because employment of a technique is one of the main aspects in which man differs fundamentally from nature.

Krimsky (1982) points out that initially molecular scientists proudly announced that they had succeeded in 'breaching the species barriers'. Later, from 1976 on, proponents of genetic engineering avoided the term, and even denied that such a thing like species barriers exists at all.

In nature generally a new species cannot come into existence by species hybridization, because that would be contradictory with the current biological definition of a species: a group of organisms with the same characteristics and properties which do breed mutually, but not with individuals of another group (species): an exclusive reproduction unit.

More to the point: natural DNA exchange between organisms of different species occurs only when they are taxonomically -very- close, possessing slight differences in their genomes, and moreover mainly in the lower orders of nature. Natural reproduction is essentially conservative; the built-in species barriers hold too much variation in check. The technique of genetic manipulation makes it possible to breach those barriers which nature generally tries to hold and preserve: in this respect genetic manipulation cannot be considered a natural process.

Of course, evolution never could occur without some mechanism for changing hereditary factors. It does so by way of mutation. Contrary to genetic engineering it is always undirected and arbitrary, however. Most mutations are lethal or not viable in the given environment. They will only replace the original characteristics of the organism when replacement gives them some competition advantage over its kin, be it by better adaptability to the environment, by resistance to infections, by more progeny, or other traits. Natural selection and selection practised by plant and cattle breeders are incomparable, in the sense that the latter needs a controlled environment for the development of the organisms.

1.2. Moral Argumentation

Thus the empirical 'naturalness' of genetic engineering leaves much to be desired. What about the normative approach? Natural Law, whereto man is subject, does not imply that everything natural is good in the moral sense. Nature does not know of good and evil, nature is nonmoral. It is only we humans who have the self-imposed duty to account for our actions. But self-imposed or not, it is man as moral actor who determines and maintains the truly human community. And this community is in formal and normative aspects indissolubly allied with the natural community. Even if we should not have direct duties to nature, we have a 'metamoral obligation' (Paden, 1992) to maintain morality, which implies, in the author's opinion, giving account of our actions regarding nature.

Assuming respect is due to nature we have to assert now whether genetic engineering infringes on it. This regards both the performing of genetic engineering and the result, the transgenic animal. I shall treat these two aspects separately.

A. genetic engineering as a purpose: the result

B. genetic engineering as an action: the means to reach the end.

12.A. Genetic engineering as a purpose: the transgenic animal[3]
*B*efore I develop my axiological argumentation I first have to elaborate on the concept of the nature *of the animal*. Again I take only vertebrate animals in consideration, without implying that my reasoning only holds good for them.

1.2.A.1. Nature of the animal
The 'nature of the animal', meaning its essence, its typical characteristics according to its taxonomical group, is the exception to the rule that nature is a dualistic concept: it has no counterpart in non-nature. Every other meaning of nature has its opposite, from the *physis/techne* dichotomy of Aristotle and the fenomenal/noumenal world of Kant to the pairs: virgin/cultivated, natural/artificial, nature/nurture, and many others.
In this sense 'nature' never is used for non-living things. Also moral consideration is restricted to biotic nature. Having a life of its own is the decisive difference between this category and the category of abiotic nature (and artifacts). Biotic and abiotic nature have the same existential characteristics, but the former also possesses essential traits, that set them apart as living entities. Ontogenetically and phylogenetically those traits appear at the individual and the collective level of biological classification respectively.
Prereflectively all and every kind of living organisms are not considered to be on the same level of moral relevance. But their status of living being, something we do not quite understand and are not able (yet) to manufacture[4], intuitively claims protection from harm. With artifacts we have less -moral- scruples: anything made by man is his to do with it like he pleases. We do have moral duties *with regard to* artifacts, however, but no direct duties *to* it; this is a more or less generally accepted ethical norm. What this means to 'living artifacts', like transgenic animals are sometimes called, will be topic of discussion next.

1.2.A.2. Moral status of transgenic animals
The author finds the foundation of his moral consideration of animals in biocentric ethics. This is based on his appreciation of the moral status of animals translated into their intrinsic value. This value acts like a moral substrate, to which may be added several second order values. I see no reason why the living artifact, the transgenic animal, should not deserve the same respect. It has also a life of its own, without regards for its use by mankind, intrinsic value included. Although transgenic animals are manufactured solely for the purpose of fulfilling our wishes and desires, mostly without any benefit for the animal itself, it does not give us the right to treat them like artifacts. This kind of genetic manipulation must lead to further instrumentalization of the animal.
In literature on animal ethics sometimes the clause 'diminished intrinsic value' is found, expressing the result of increased instrumentalization, as if the one increases at the cost of the other. I consider this idea false, because in my opinion intrinsic value is a categorical and absolute value. It is an innate property of every animal, an 'essential characteristic' in the Feyerabendian sense[5]. This is difficult to explain in objective terms, because essence only can be experienced. As Feyerabend

(ibidem) explains: "This experience consists in the presence of a mental picture, a sensation, a phenomenon, a feeling, or a inner process of a more etheral kind." Therefore I think it is not appropriate to call a transgenic animal a case of 'diminished intrinsic value'. The situation or condition in which the animal finds itself is totally irrelevant in this respect: ill, imprisoned, newborn or aged, invalid, transgenic or manipulated otherwise, domesticated, nothing can influence the intrinsic value in a positive or negative way. 'The river remains the same, wherever it flows, although quality or quantity of the water may vary'. At most a variation regards the amount of moral relevance and consideration. That is why I postulate that the nature of transgenic animals deserves just the same measure of protection that is enjoyed by the other animals.

1.2.B. Genetic engineering as an acion: the means and the end
In normative ethics not only the purpose of one's actions count, but the means by which to reach the end too. When our acting concerns entities with intrinsic value, they have to be in proportion to this end. Therefore I now shall analyze critically and evaluate morally the performance of genetic engineering itself. This may or may not be in relation with the purpose, be it animal production, scientific knowledge, domestication, veterinary or other goals.

Can an action by itself be valued as morally good or bad? Or more to the point: can any technique be evaluated as such? Technology generally is considered to be morally neutral: it is the end to which it is used that retrospectively decides the morality of the act. Nevertheless we know of many secondary and often unintentional results of technology that may unequivocally be judged as bad. For example the genetic techniques by which the 'Green Revolution' provided high yields of maize and rice, at the other hand caused many problems like salination of the fields, poverty of small farmers, unemployment, and lowered resistance to pests. Many other examples can be given.

But can we call genetic engineering a morally objectionable technique *as such*? Is it ethically reprehensible to change the genome, and with it a couple of characteristics of an animal? We are not allowed to use the naturalistic argument here, like we demonstrated *supra*, and cannot use the historical argument either, like will be proved *infra*. Which leads to the conclusion, for lack of any other relevant arguments, that genetic engineering must be considered like any other kind of technique: morally neutral, in retrospect depending on the end and the contingent secondary effects. That will mean restrictions to the application of this technique, to be discussed next.

1.2.B.1. Animal rights
To analyze these restrictions genetic engineering must be evaluated according to specific moral criteria, which can be translated into moral rights of animal subjects. These may be formulated as follows:
- the right of a life unfolding according to its nature
- that is a life in a natural and social environment giving optimal satisfaction
- especially, a life devoid of human interference not in the interest of the subject.

So the question is: does our acting, c.q. using genetic engineering, interferes with animal life in a measure that their fundamental rights are violated?

With respect to the nature of the animal I think we must ascertain that genetic engineering, by transgressing the species barriers, facilitates to a degree a more or less radical change of this nature. And by changing the nature, which change moreover is hereditary, one is demonstrating a lack of respect to the animal-as-it-is by manipulating it into an animal-as-we-want. This is another way of saying that we irreversibly instrumentalize the animal, which is incompatible with its intrinsic value. It is the nature of the animal, its essential being, that we generally value most. Before finishing the part of the naturalistic argument I like to give a short analysis of two other restrictions to genetic engineering to complete the picture. They deal with animal suffering and with environmental exploitation which affects especially animals.

1.2.B.2. Suffering
It is a truism that making an animal suffer is not in its interest. Insofar as genetic engineering is the cause of suffering it can be easily diasapproved of, provided it is not the result of veterinary measures meant to cure the animal. In the practice of genetic engineering suffering by direct manipulation is negligible, because the object is the gamete or early embryo, which are considered not to feel any pain, as far as we know, let alone they can suffer. But because of the -still- very experimental character of this technique anything can go wrong, which not seldom it does. Many animals must be sacrificed to get the desired results; in known experiments with cattle it is not uncommon to get more than 90% of the transgenic animals showing all kinds of defects and deficiencies (Pursel, et al., 1989; Broom, 1995), not to mention the countless faulty experiments that even fail to result in offspring.

1.2.B.3. Exploitation of nature
Many human activities can threaten life without greatly disturbing the individual animal. Interventions directed to nature development and reclamation are disturbing and unbalancing the ecosystem indirectly. Several (animal) species are getting into trouble, some are becoming extinct. Individual suffering cannot be excluded, but the main disadvantage is that life sustenance is becoming worse and the animals may disappear entirely. The effect is the same as killing the animals directly. The practice of genetic engineering may have the same effect, especially when transgenic animals are released into the wild. Although this is practised mainly with transgenic plants, for animals holds the same. When we manipulate animals expressly for putting them back into nature it only makes sense if they have a competition advantage to their kin. Otherwise they will never survive in a rather stable ecosystem. By this advantage they are able to and will repress and eventually drive out other species, which may cause the extinction of the latter.

Concluding this section on the naturalistic argument the author ascertains that, apart from argumentation errors, there are fundamental objections to the comparison between genetic engineering and the workings of nature. The main moral arguments are that genetic engineering may *violate* the nature of the animal and furthers its instrumentalization if it is used only for changing it according to our wishes and desires. Those changes do not occur in nature, and are in this respect unnatural. If they do, why would we not prefer and use them, like we do by upgrading through breeding and selection, in stead of using genetic engineering? Secondary objections can be raised against the technique as such when it causes suffering of the experimental animal or its progeny, and when it is instrumental to the disturbing of the ecosystem by populating it with transgenic animals.

2. The historical argument

Much of what has been contended in the part of the naturalistic argument has also relevance to this part. The comparison between genetic engineering and nature is here replaced by genetic engineering and classical breeding, *i.e.* the historical argument. This argumentation follows the line of the historical justification of genetic engineering, because since times immemorial mankind has improved its lifestock by crossing and selecting favourable traits. And genetic engineering is only considered a better way, because it is quicker and more efficient.

On nearer scrutiny, however, this appears not to be the case. Crossings of -domestic- animals never crossed successfully the species barriers; when exceptions occur (horses X donkeys, different species of ducks) they are infertile. But also the *process* of genetic engineering is not alike normal breeding. The offspring of crossings is the result of the pairing and uniting of two gametes (which is more than their total DNA contents), while in transgenesis the progeny itself is the subject of artificial hybridization: one or more (parts of) DNA strands are transferred to an early embryo, which is manipulated by way of eliminating more or less comparable strands of their own DNA; or the gamete is entirely denucleated like in cloning. Classic breeding, just like nature itself, does not work with 'donors' and 'acceptors', but always with the whole genome.

2.1. Moral Argumentation

This special case of the historical argument is obviously empirically false. What about the general character of this reasoning? Historic arguments often take no account of the constraints of time and place. Morals and norms differ from culture to culture, and change in time as well. In history we always encounter cases that are ambiguous or even contradictory. People using arguments derived from a historical fact often mean: *our* history. That is not to deny historical trends exist; in this connection we may refer to the domestication of wild animals, a subject I shall treat later on.

Ethically speaking the historical argument has no moral value *per se*. Situations that were accepted or approved of formerly, are now forcefully denounced: slavery, child labour, discrimination of race, sex, and others. And the beforementioned natural fallacy sometimes falls back on historical reasons as well, because we see nature as something eternal, unchangeable and therefore factually good (which does not have to be the same as morally good).

2.2. Factory Farming

An impressive change of public opinion has been demonstrated in the case of factory farming. There is a growing public opposition to this practice, and not only in the Netherlands, where we decided to kill nearly two million newborn piglets to counter an outbreak of swine pest. Not only vegetarians join the opposition, but many people become convinced that the animal in our care has a right to a better life, a life according to its nature. Policy intentions of a new arrangement of swine meat production by the Dutch Ministry of Agriculture point in this direction.

We may approach the problem of factory farming from quite another direction: the genetic engineering solution. Why not manipulate genetically to get a new breed of cattle, to replace the rather crude measures we have to take to prevent animals living according to their nature? We can *change* their nature, can't we? We may be able to manifacture cows without horns, swine and cats without genitals, we may forsake in an elegant way troublesome claws, tails, and ears. Eventually Rollin's warning for future living egg machines (Rollin, 1995) without feeling, instead of cumbersome chickens who need air, light, a place to scratch the ground, and room for flapping their wings, may become reality. But do we want this kind of solution?

2.3. Domestication

The historical argument leads us to consider also the position of the domesticated animal more closely. In the history of mankind domestication of wild animals has always been an ongoing trend. Without doubt domestication changes the animal's nature, on purpose, by being captured, confined, and tamed, needing human presence for their wellbeing and care. It would be absurd to de-domesticate our cattle and pets, even if we were able to. But they have a nature of their own too, like wild animals, and the same right of moral consideration. We do not have the right to treat them only as objects. Out of respect for intrinsic value, in the author's opinion, we have to stop further domestication of animals, violating their nature and making them more dependent on us. That goes for wild species as well.

3. The 'no, unless...'-policy

To conclude: the historical argument does not succeed in convincing me more of its validity as does the naturalistic one. It is neither empirically sound, nor gives it satisfactory normative arguments to prolong and extend practices like factory farming and domestication. Does this mean we have to reject genetic engineering entirely?

That should mean that genetic engineering is intrinsically morally evil, but that again is in contradiction with my statement that every technique is morally neutral. It also would mean that transgenic animals have no right to exist, whatever the reason they were given life. Of course the proponents of genetic engineering are right in this respect that genetic engineering is a technique, a scientific proceeding by which we can alter the genetic make-up of animals. But not without restrictions, like I described before, we owe to the animal because of its intrinsic value.

That is the reason the author pleads in favour for the Dutch animal protection laws that, acknowledging the intrinsic value of animals, forbid genetic engineering[6]. To get an exemption one has to indicate good reasons for performing it, mere instrumental reasons are not enough. This is the so called 'no, unless'-policy.

This formula was chosen because there are wide-felt serious objections to genetic engineering. But it is no absolute ban. The 'no, unless...policy' does not exclude a positive and morally sound use of genetic engineering in the case of gene therapy, when the animal is constrained by its genetic heritage to use its potential fully. Also experiments are allowed where overwhelming human interests are at stake, depending approval of an Ethical Board (like every animal experiment in the Netherlands). Intrinsic value is considered as a *prima facie* principle, and can be overruled by other important interests for good reasons, like in some cases when human intrinsic value is at stake. In my opinion experiments that change the nature of the animal, however, ought never be allowed.

Conclusion

Genetic engineering gives mankind undreamt of possibilities to improve on nature, but not everthing possible is also morally allowed. Neither naturalistic nor historical arguments suffice to treat genetic manipulation exactly the same as any other experimental technique. I conclude that not genetic engineering itself, but mainly when it leads to changing the nature of the animal, must be considered as an expression of disrespect for the animal's intrinsic value, and accordingly must be condemned.
In nature survival means flexibility, diversity, adaptability of the animals or their species; the 'nature of the animal', be it domestic or wild, must be kept intact to be able to employ these characteristics. Genetic engineering aims for predictability and uniformity, which is only possible in an entirely controlled and invariant environment, that is very vulnerable to technical failures. At the end we threaten to find ourselves in a wholly man-made world, devoid of anything natural, where we shall not recognize ourselves anymore. Maybe this futuristic picture expresses another very strong reason why we have to proceed with genetic engineering with the utmost carefulness.

Notes

1. This paper deals only with vertbrate animals, because they are the main object of genetic manipulation nowadays, which raises fundamental moral questions.
2. "...und die Berufung auf die Natur ist (...) wo es um Handlungen geht, keine Begründung. Wer Gene manipuliert, macht *nicht* das Gleiche wie die Natur, sondern dadurch, dasz er es *macht*, ist es nicht das Gleiche." (Löw, 1983).
3. see note 1.
4. What is a reason to abstain (*i.e.* interfering with life) for the one, is for the other a challenge trying to unveil the secret of life. And genetic engineering may contribute to that end.
5. "An essential characteriastic is in practice nomore than a 'family of cases'; a 'complicated network of similarities, overlapping and criss-crossing'" *(Problems of Empiricism,* p.100).
6. Act of Animal Health and Wellbeing, 1992. *Animal Experimentation Act,* 1977/1996.

Literature

- Broom, D.M. (1995).Measuring the Effect of Management, Methods, Systems, High Production Efficiency and Biotechnology on Farm Animal Welfare, in T.B. Mepham, G.A. Tucker and J. Wiseman (eds.). *Issues in Agricultural Bioethics* (pp. 319-334). Nottingham: University of Nottingham Press.
- Feyerabend, P.K. (1981). *Problems of Empiricism,* Philosophical Papers, Vol. 2 (pp. 100-102). Cambridge: Cambridge University Press.
- Krimsky, S. (1982). *Genetic Alchemy - The Social History of the Recombinant DNA Cntroversy,* (p. 264). Cambridge (Mass.): The MIT Press.
- Löw, R. (1983). Gen und Ethik. Philosophische Überlegungen zum Umgang mit menschlichen Erbgut, in J. Koslowski, P. Kreuzer und R. Löw (eds.). *Die Verführung durch das Machbare.* Stuttgart: S. Hirschel Verlag.
- Paden, R. (1992). Nature and Morality. *Environmental Ethics* 14/3, 239-252.
- Pursel, V.G., Pinkert C.A., Miller K.F., Bolt D.J., Campbell R.G., Palmiter R.D., Brinster R.L. & Hammer E. (1989). Genetic Engineering of Livestock. *Science* 224, 1281-1288.
- Rollin, B.E. (1995).*The Frankenstein Syndrome: Ethical and Social Issues in Genetic Engineering of Animals.* (pp. 172-175). Cambridge: Cambridge University Press, 1995.

6
Bio-ethics and the intrinsic value of animals

Henk Verhoog

Institute of Evolutionary and Ecological Sciences
Leiden University, NL

1. Introduction

This contribution is meant to be a retrospect to the other chapters of this part ("The intrinsic value of animals: ethical issues"). In one way or another the authors of these chapters struggle with the relationship between (factual) knowledge about living organisms, and the morality of our relation to these organisms. The central concepts of these chapters (naturality, species-specific behaviour, autonomy and integrity) are all used with both moral and biological connotations, with the concept of the intrinsic value of animals as a unifying category. It can have this function as a unifying category because of its key meaning: having a value of its own, by itself, independent of its usefulness (its instrumental value) for human beings.
This reference to the autonomous being of an animal is not without complications, especially of a meta-ethical kind. Speaking about 'intrinsic' value (or 'inherent' worth) suggests that this value is an objective value. It is sometimes formulated by environmental or animal ethicists as if such a value has an objective existence, comparable to the existence of a natural property of an animal. Those who emphasize the human side of the valuing process sometimes go to another extreme. All valuation, they say, is a human, subjective activity. References to the external world do and should not play any role in the moral justification of human behaviour. Values, it is said, can not be derived from facts (naturalistic fallacy). In this retrospect an attempt has been made to shed some light on these issues, at the same time trying to keep as close as possible to the topics dealt with in the other contributions. A suggestion is made of how the central concepts of these chapters can be classified in a coherent way.

2. The domain of bio-ethics

In english-speaking countries 'bio-ethics' is usually defined as the (philosophical) study of the moral questions related to any interference in the lives of human beings. The 'bio' in bio-ethics refers to the biological aspects of being human, or of human beings. In the Netherlands the *Dutch Society of Bio-ethics* uses a broader definition, including other living organisms as well (animals in particular). The latter definition reflects developments in the last decades, in which animals (animal ethics) and nature as a whole (environmental ethics) have become serious objects of moral reflection.

It is not possible here to recapitulate these developments in detail. The emphasis will be on the changes taking place in the meaning of 'intrinsic value' (see also Visser & Verhoog, 1986, and Verhoog, 1992). The term 'intrinsic value' was originally applied to certain conscious experiences of human beings. In most systems of traditional ethics only human beings have moral relevance. These ethics deal with relations between humans only. This is nowadays called a basic *anthropocentric* attitude. Intrinsic values refer to the highest qualities of human experience (such as life, health, freedom etc.). These values can not be derived from something else (nonderivative values). It is therefore said that they are 'good or worthwile in themselves'. Values which contribute to, or are instrumental to the attainment of intrinsic values are called extrinsic values. In the anthropocentric view, animals and nature in general can only have an extrinsic value for man, they have no intrinsic value.

According to Frankena (1963) intrinsic values are contributive to 'the intrinsically good life' of human beings. He distinguishes between the intrinsically good life nd the morally good life. A morally good life means living in agreement with certain ethical principles or moral intentions; this only applies to moral agents. The morally good life is directed at the realisation of the intrinsically good life. When human autonomy or freedom is seen as intrinsically good than it automatically follows that we have to respect this freedom.

The next step in the development was that the scope of the term intrinsic value was enlarged and applied to (the experiences of) 'higher' animals as well. Higher animals that can experience pain (sentient animals) necessarily must have some form of conscious awareness. As a reaction to the purely instrumental use of animals in modern society opponents of intensive husbandry and animal experimentation began to use the term in contrast to 'instrumental', to indicate that animals have 'a value of their own'. The focus shifted to the view that animals are more or less autonomous entities with 'a good of their own'. The term 'autonomy' is used in this context to emphasize the relative independence of animals; it is not meant to be similar to human autonomy.

In a later publication Frankena (1979) says in this regard: "I can see no reason, from the moral point of view, why we should respect something that is alive but has no conscious sentience and can so experience no pleasure or pain, joy or suffering, unless it is perhaps potentially a conscious sentient being, as in the case of a fetus." (p.11). For Frankena only the experiences and lives of conscious individual sentient beings (including higher animals) can have intrinsic value. This conclusion is shared by several well-known animal ethicists, such as Singer (1975), Rollin (1981) and Regan (1984).

I will use the term *zoocentric* ethics when the concept of intrinsic value is thus applied to sentient animals. In the zoocentric approach moral agents have to show respect to all sentient beings because the absence of pain and the enjoyment of pleasure is believed to be intrinsically good for these animals. Some adherents to this approach only admit apes into the moral domain, others extend it to all vertebrates (including fishes). It is not surprising that the discussion focuses on domestic animals, animals which stand in a particular relation of dependence to human beings. Wild animals are included as long as they are sentient, and as long as the well-being of individual animals is at issue. In many moral codes and laws, such as the Dutch law on animal experimentation, this zoocentric ethics is accepted. The emphasis is on vertebrate animals and the prevention of pain.

In the zoocentric approach concepts developed within an anthropocentric context are extended to those animals which are closest to human beings. The way the concept of intrinsic value is used illustrates this. What is intrinsically valuable *for* the animal depends on certain conscious experiences of the animal. This should be distinguished from the intrinsic value *of* the animal itself. What is intrinsically valuable for the animals may vary (experiences may be more or less intrinsically valuable). But all animals having such experiences have intrinsic value in an absolutistic sense (no degrees).

The next extension of the domain of bio-ethics is the *biocentric* view. In this view not only sentient creatures but all living beings have intrinsic value. The biocentric outlook on nature developed by Taylor (1986) is a good example of this. In this outlook all organisms have an 'inherent worth', because they are "teleological centers of life in the sense that each is a unique individual pursuing its own good in its own way" (100). This means for Taylor that moral agents ought to respect all living organisms, not only sentient animals. Because the concept of intrinsic value is traditionally associated with subjective human experience (in the sense described above: intrinsically valuable experiences), Taylor speaks about 'inherent worth'. He wants to make clear that he does not speak about the value of an experience for certain lliving beings (sentient animals) but about an absolute value (without degrees) which ois applicable to all life. Taylor (1984) gives the following definition of 'inherent worth': "Inherent worth is the value something has simply in virtue of the fact that it has a good of its own. To say that an entity has inherent worth is to say that its good (welfare, well-being) is deserving of the concern and consideration of all moral agents and that the realization of its good is something to be promoted or protected as an end in itself and for the sake of the being whose good it is." (151)

Taylor argues that all living beings are 'teleological centers of life' and therefore it is only with reference to living beings that it makes sense to speak of promoting or protecting their well-being and doing this for their own sake.

From the anthropocentric to the biocentric view we see a progressive widening of the moral domain (we leave out the ecocentric view here). Although the 'good' may be different for all these natural entities, the fact that they have a good of their own (in contrast to non-living entities) brings them into the moral sphere. That they have a good of their own means that what moral agents do to them is not indifferent to the existence and well-being of these entities.

3. Instrumental and intrinsic value

It is assumed in this contribution that 'valuation' always refers to (expresses) a relation between human beings and some object which is valued. One can also say that a relation only comes into existence when valuation is involved. 'Moral' valuation occurs when the object has a good of its own. This means that having a good of its own is a necessary, though not sufficient condition for moral considerability. We have no moral obligations to an X, when this X has no good of its own. The reverse is not necessarily true: the fact that something has a good of its own does not logically imply that we have moral obligations towards this object. It is further assumed here that all living entities have a good of their own. From now onwards when I talk about 'valuation' I will mean moral valuation.

Valuation always involves both a human being as subject and an object which is valued. When the focus is on the human being, the object valued is said to have an *instrumental value*. It is instrumental/contributive to the realisation of an intrinsic value of human beings. When, in valuation, the human being is focusing on the object for its own sake (because it has a good of its own), then the *intrinsic value* of the object is emphasized. The relation is non-instrumental in this case. It is important to realize that both instrumental and intrinsic value are defined here as relational terms [1]. Notice further that in the formulation chosen the concept of intrinsic value is not derived from any specific properties of the object concerned, except the general property of 'having a good of its own'.

In the anthropocentric view non-human living entities are not included in the moral domain, and therefore they cannot have an intrinsic value. They only can have an instrumental value. In the zoocentric view only those natural entities are included in the moral domain which are more or less similar to human beings as far as conscious experience is concerned. Although this view is not 'anthropocentric' in the strict sense of the term, it may be argued that the concept of intrinsic value used is derived from the anthropocentric view (Verhoog & Visser, 1997). Because of the emphasis on the animal's consciousness, the existence of human consciousness is taken as paradigmatic for having intrinsic value. The specific forms of animal conscious experience are compared with the conscious experience of human beings. Human consciousness is taken to be the standard, on the basis of which lower and higher forms of consciousness are distinguished. This usually leads to unsatisfying discussions about borderlines within the animal kingdom, and between animal consciousness and human consciousness.

In the biocentric view all living beings (for practical purposes all plants and animals) can have both instrumental and intrinsic value for human beings. That is the reason why it is sometimes said that attributing intrinsic value to animals or other organisms brings them into the moral domain. Having intrinsic value is then dependent on and inseperable from the act of moral valuation. This view has several important consequences for the question of the subjective and objective aspects of intrinsic value.

4. Subjectivity and objectivity in relation to intrinsic value

The view that the attribution of intrinsic value is not derived from any facts about the animals concerned, but is an inherent aspect of the relation expressed by moral valuing itself, implies that the meta-ethical discussion about the question whether intrinsic value is an 'objective' value or not, takes quite a different turn.

O'Neill (1992) distinguished three different senses of the term intrinsic value:
1. non-instrumental value, end in itself;

2. the value an object has solely in virtue of its intrinsic (non-relational) properties;
3. the value an object possesses independently of the evaluation of valuers ('objective value').

The discussion about the objectivity or subjectivity of values (the so-called objective value concept) is a meta-ethical discussion about the origin of value-judgments and about their justification. The third meaning distinguished by O'Neill contradicts my definition of attributing (moral) value to something. When it is accepted that the term 'value' always refers to a relation between a subject which attributes value and an object to which the value is attributed, then objective values as defined by O'Neill simply do not exist. We have to transcend this form of dualism between subjectivism and objectivism. Values are neither purely subjective, nor purely objective, there is always an element of both in them. If this is true for values in general, then it must also be true for the specific category of intrinsic values.

Human beings may value something instrumentally if it is useful for them, if it increases their well-being (or any other state of body or mind which is said to be of intrinsic value) in one way or another. What is believed to be of intrinsic value may be formulated both in a subjective way (now defined as how it feels for a certain person) and in an objective way (on the basis of some theory about the 'good life' of human beings). The former may be called a first-person perspective and the latter a third-person perspective on intrinsic values.

A third-person perspective may lead to the ordering of values in some value-theory. Such a theory abstracts from the (subjective) 'feels' or preferences of a particular person or group in search of what is good for human beings in a more general (objective) sense. In both the first-person perspective and the third-person perspective the highest values, which can no longer be seen as instrumental to the achievement of other values, are sometimes called ends-in-themselves, or intrinsic values. The word 'intrinsic value' is then used in O'Neill's first sense (non-instrumental value).

The question now is whether it is also possible to talk about a moral value-theory (formulated by humans) in relation to (particular species of) animals. Once animals are included in the moral domain (because they have a good-of-their-own) it is legitimate to ask the question what is of intrinsic value to these animals. In the utilitarian approach of Singer and Rollin the absence of pain and the experience of pleasure are believed to be of intrinsic value to sentient animals. This is based on what animals feel from a first-person perspective. Animals without conscious experiences cannot have intrinsic-value-experiences according to this utilitarian approach. In this approach, to have a good of their own is not enough for inclusion whin the moral domain, the animals must themselves be aware of what matters to them, they must 'feel' it somehow.

For human beings it always remains difficult to really know what is going on in the mind of animals from the first-person perspective. From a preference-utilitarian perspective we can try to find out what kind of living conditions are prefered by the animals themselves (giving them the possibility to choose). We can also come to a better understanding of what is going on in animals by direct interaction and communication with animals. This may be called the second-person perspective; the animal is not objectified as an object of scientific research, but is treated as a partner. Some say that even on the basis of the third-person perspective it is possible to say something about the quality of life of animals, about what is of value to them in an objective sense.[2]

Although all valuation is a human activity, there is always an 'objective' element involved in it. We can talk about valuation from my own personal experience, but we can also ask what is valuable *for* human beings, or *for* animals of a particular kind. Intrinsic values were considered to be the highest values *for* these beings, either subjectively or objectively. It will be clear by now that to decide which values are 'intrinsic' in this sense (non-instrumental: O'Neill's first meaning) we have to know something about the characteristic nature, or properties of the beings involved. This holds both for the zoocentric view, which opens the moral domain for sentient animals only, as for the biocentric view. The difference between the zoocentric and the biocentric view is that in the biocentric view it is not required for an animal to be sentient to be included into the moral domain. In the biocentric view one can speak about the 'good' of animals independent of the question whether the animals consciously experience what is good to/for them.

5. Intrinsic value and the nature of animals

It is time for a short recapitulation of the steps in the argumentation. To have a good of its own is a necessary condition for being admitted to the moral domain. Being admitted to the moral domain implies that the entities concerned stand in a relation of moral valuation to human beings. All such entities have both instrumental *and* intrinsic value for human beings. This means that such entities can not be used as 'mere instruments'. When the latter occurs, as in the anthropocentric view, then these entities are factually excluded from the moral domain. What does it mean for human beings to acknowledge that animals have an intrinsic value? It means that the 'good' (short form of 'having a good of its own') of these animals must be taken into account. To be able to realize this we must develop a theory of the good of the animals concerned; we must know what is of intrinsic value to the animals themselves.

What is of intrinsic value for the animals themselves is morally relevant *because of* the acknowledgement of the intrinsic value of the animals as end-in-themselves; the moral relevance is not derived from any factual knowledge about these animals. The importance of the latter distinction becomes clear when we look at O'Neill's second meaning of intrinsic value: the value an object has because of its intrinsic (non-relational) properties. My first objection to this wording is that it suggests that the intrinsic value of animals is 'derived' from the properties they have. As indicated, I would like to reverse this; their properties are morally relevant because of the inclusion of these animals in the moral domain. My second objection is related to the equalization of intrinsic properties with non-relational properties. Non-relationality should not be brought in here, but in an earlier stage of the argumentation.

When we say that animals themselves have intrinsic value we usually mean that animals not only have an instrumental value for human beings, but also have a value-of-their-own, an intrinsic value ('non-relationality' meaning: not related to human interests). They do not exist solely for the purpose of being useful to human beings; they have an intrinsic value because they have a good of their own. The non-relationality does not refer to any specific characteristics of a certain species of animals. Of a real instrument we can say that it was made (created) by man to use it for some purpose; it cannot have an intrinsic value in the non-relational meaning of the term. Even domestic animals have not been made by man in the same sense. They have been changed through selection and training, but it is still possible to say of these animals that they have a value-of-their-own, a good life of their own, in spite of all these changes.

We have seen that moral valuation establishes a relation between a (human) subject and an object of which it can be said that it has a good of its own. When the relation is only focussed upon the 'good' of the subject, then we speak about a purely instrumental relation. For the subject the object only has an instrumental value. When the object is cared for as an end in itself, for its own sake, then the relation is non-instrumental. In the case of animals the focus would then only be on the animal's good of its own, irrespective of the animals' use to human beings. Many people have experienced this in wild-life observation. One may argue that human beings do this for selfish reasons (enjoyment, aesthetic reasons) and that, therefore, it is not a non-instrumental relation. Such an argument is still based on the dualistic (either-or) conception of valuation. When someone rescues a child from drowning, and is glad or proud about it afterwards, then we will not in general say that the rescuer only did this to get feelings of gladness.

O'Neill uses the example of friendship to illustrate an 'Aristotelean attempt to bridge the logical gap between facts and oughts', as if the only way of defending that I ought to protect the flourishing of a friend of mine (or any other object with a good of its own), would be that this flourishing is constitutive of my own flourishing. When moral valuing is interpreted in a non-dualistic framework it is not necessary to argue in this way. When an instrumental and a non-instrumental relation are seen as two possibilities inherent in any moral valuation, then it could just as well be said that being fully or really 'human' ought to involve the attempt/ or duty to love more and more beings for their own sake. Not as a legitimation for unselfish behaviour in the past, but as a free choice, as a goal to strive after. That is how I understand it now when we attribute intrinsic value to animals. It means that we step outside the anthropocentric perspective by our free choice, in an attempt to create a better balance between our own interests and the interests of animals. Once the step towards a more biocentric view on animals and nature has been made, with the intrinsic value of animals as our moral beacon, the search for an answer to the question of what it means for a specific animal to have a good of its own becomes unavoidable. To try to come to a deeper understanding of concepts such as the 'nature' of the animal, its species-specific behaviour and its integrity then becomes a real challenge.

6. Naturality, species-specificity and integrity

In a radical anthropocentric view animals do not count morally, except as instruments for the fulfillment of human purposes. In an extreme biocentric view human beings are not allowed to interfere in nature, out of respect for the intrinsic value of nature. Being aware of these extremes is useful, because certain tendencies in our culure can be better understood, when seen in relation to these extremes. We can recognise tendencies going in one way or another. The tendency to interfere in and to control nature is one tendency. A good example is the increasing control over animal (and human) procreation, with selective breeding, artificial insemination, in vitro fertilisation, embryo transplantation, genetic modification and cloning as successive steps in this process. One way of reacting against this increasing control over the animal's lives is to say that it is 'unnatural', or 'artificial'. Opponents of this process see the patenting of genetically modified organisms as the final step. In the past only human inventions could be patented, artifacts. Patenting living beings as if they are mere 'compositions of matter' makes these animals into human constructs, developed for purely instrumental reasons.

We also see the other tendency, as a reaction to the increasing instrumentalisation of animals in intensive husbandry and animal experimentation. In ecological (biological) agriculture in particular, the aim is to make agriculture more 'natural', taking into account ecological principles and the 'nature' of the animals.

A good illustration of this biocentric approach is an article by Bartussek (1991) in which he comes to a gradation of 'naturalness' in animal production. Soil management, animal husbandry techniques, animal breeding programmes and animal feeding systems are graded on a scale with the following grades: natural, near to nature, not near to nature, far off nature and unnatural/industrialized. There is a more biocentric attitude prevailing here. In the Netherlands we even see that former agricultural areas are 'given back to nature'; this is called 'nature restoration'. The main idea behind it is that modern agricultural practice is one of the main reasons for the loss of biological diversity. The motive behind nature development is partly human-centred (the joy of experiencing biological diversity, or 'wilderness'), partly nature-centred (because of the intrinsic value of plant- and animal species).

The chapter by Visser (this volume) about 'The incompatibility of intrinsic value with genetic manipulation' deals with the moral relevance of the concept of 'naturality' in relation to the genetic modification of animals. Arguments in which the morality of human action (say the genetic modification of animals) is defended by appealing to the fact that it is natural to do so (in agreement with the laws of nature), or that it occurs in nature as well, are rejected as cases of the naturalistic fallacy. A dualistic, either-or, approach (it is either nature or culture, etc.) is not very fruitful. The view, however, that any reference to what is natural is forbidden (because of the naturalistic fallacy), is not correct. The use of this argument often coincides with an anthropocentric view upon nature.

I tried to demonstrate that it is possible to choose freely for a biocentric view, in which the moral domain is enlarged to all entities having 'a good of their own'. And, as Visser shows, this leads to the moral relevance of the 'nature' of the animal, its character, its essence, which we have to take into account if we want to apply the biocentric moral attitude in practice. It also makes it possible to speak about grades of naturality with respect to domestic animals. Systems of animal husbandry can be more or less natural, that is close to the needs and nature of the animals involved. It is not the same as deriving our moral principles (telling us what we 'ought' to do) from nature.

If I understand him well, also Van den Bos, in the chapter about species-specific behaviour, comes to the same conclusion, although his argumentation differs. It is a moral choice to what extent we want to take the intrinsic value of animals into account when we use animals instrumentally. We first have to recognize the intrinsic value of animals. This implies that we first have to decide whether the goal that we want to use the animals for is an important goal and that there are no alternative ways to reach this goal. After it has been decided that this is the case 'we have to do our best to safeguard the animals' perspectives and interests'. Then several moral principles come into play: care for health and welfare, respect for the animal's integrity, and respect for the animal's naturalness.

What is the relation between these moral principles and intrinsic value? To answer this we have to return to our starting point. We said that in a relation of moral valuation the object of valuation must have a good of its own (independent of its usefulness for human beings). The concept of intrinsic value emphasizes this good of its own, tries to capture its meaning. It stresses the 'otherness' of the being involved, tries to understand this otherness for its own sake. When the other being is an animal we can at least ask three questions (see also Verhoog, 1997):

1. what does it mean to be an animal?
2. what does it mean to be an animal of this kind (species)?
3. what is this individual animal, belonging to this species?

The question what it means to be an animal lies at a rather abstract level. It is rarely asked by the scientists themselves. For philosophers of nature or ethicists it is an important question in a comparative sense. The question of the difference between plants and animals for instance, or between animals and human beings is asked in the philosophy of biology and in philosophical antropology.

An essay by Kasanmoentalib (1994) gives an impression of what kind of answers we might get from the field of philosophical biology/anthropology. The hermeneutic biologists/philosophers she deals with (Portmann, Plessner and Von Weizsäcker) all question the cartesian dichotomy between subject and object, identifying human nature with subjectivity (consciousness, etc.) and the rest of nature with objectivity (material existence). They use different concepts to express the autonomy and centricity ('subjectness', being a self) of all living organisms, and animals in particular. The very principle that all living organisms have a 'good of their own' gets meaning from this perspective.

What it means to be an animal has been made much more concrete by Wemelsfelder (1997). Wemelsfelder speaks about animal behaviour, and the subjectivity of animals in general terms, also starting from a phenomenological/hermeneutic first-person perspective (recognizing that each individual animal is a 'self', actively exploring and interacting with the environment). The animal as a whole is seen as a dynamic, integrative centre of action, maintaining continuous sensory contact with the environment through processes of attention, orientation and monitoring. The flexibility and versatility of animal behaviour is best shown under natural or semi-natural conditions. These conditions are then contrasted with intensive housing systems. These systems tend to severly restrict behavioral autonomy of animals, which may lead to enduring boredom and depression. Here we see the same tension between natural and artificial (man-made) conditions. From such a reflection on the question what it means to be an animal (and not a plant) generalizable criteria of the 'good' of animals can be derived, such as awareness of the outside world (the animal's 'Umwelt'), autonomous activity, independentness. These are generalizable criteria because they apply to all species of animals, although in various ways.

The next step is that we go to the species-specific level, to try to answer the second question what it means to be an animal of a certain species. Here the concept of species-specific behaviour becomes of paramount importance (Van den Bos, this volume). When making judgements about the health and well-being of organisms (also domestic animals) veterinarians and ethologists necessarily have to refer to the species to which the animals belong. With the criteria becoming more specific we may expect the role of the biologist to become more important. From the chapter of Van den Bos it becomes clear that there are different concepts of species-specific behaviour, more or less close to our common sense experience of animal behaviour. They have in common that they all refer to behaviour which is unique, or characteristic for a particular species.

If we want to know what the good-of-its-own of an animal is, than we not only have to realize that it is an animal, but also that it belongs to a particular species, evolutionary adapted to a particular range of environments. The concept of 'species' may be defined in different ways, and it may be difficult sometimes to differentiate between species, but such taxonomic problems are not really relevant here. Also the fact that species-specific behaviour may change during the course of evolution is not really relevant in the moral context we are talking about. Evolution is a slow process of change, slow enough to speak about the stability of species-specific behaviour. And that is all we need, when we refer to the moral relevance of the nature of the organisms concerned.

These differences between species become important after it has been decided (as a consequence of attributing intrinsic value to animals) that the instrumental use of living organisms serves a substantial human goal, and that there are no alternatives to reach this goal. They can also become important when one of the alternatives involves the use of another species. In the case that there is a dilemma and we have to choose either the one, or the other species, than the choice of one of them does not mean that we do no longer respect the intrinsic value of the other one. We are not allowed to say that the one chosen has less intrinsic value than the other.

The last level distinguished by us is the level of the individual animal. Compared to plants individual variety is much stronger in animal life (Bekoff, 1994), and culminating in humans, where respect for the individual person is ingrained in most ethical systems. Animal species differ as to their 'level of individualization' (corresponding with psychological complexity). It is not a surprise that with respect to the morality of our relation to animals some people focus morality at the individual level, whereas others see it at the level of the species. The latter see species-survival as the relevant moral category, rather than the survival of individual animals. I cannot go into this discussion now. What is of importance here is that all species consist of individuals, but the level of individual complexity may be very different between these species. Just as the concept of independence (autonomy, self-regulation) gives a good characterization of the level of animality, and the concept of naturalness of the level of species-specificity, so we may say that the concept of integrity may best be used at the level of the individual animals. In the chapter by Rutgers & Heeger (this volume) an explication of this concept is given. They argue that besides criteria such as pain, health and welfare we also need the integrity-criterium to deal with human interferences such as genetic modification, castration and sterilisation of animals, ear-cropping and tail-docking in dogs, etc. Even if all these operations can be done painlessly, there is reason to think that they are not morally neutral. It is interesting to see how this concept is defined by the authors: 'the wholeness and completeness of the animal and the species-specific balance of the creature, as well as the animal's capacity to maintain itself independently in an environment suitable to the species'.

We see that the three levels distinguished in my contribution are combined by the authors in the concept of integrity. Although I prefer to apply the concept of integrity to individual animals, it is true that the other two levels are involved at this level. Every individual animal is at the same time an animal of a certain species. And therefore, the criteria that we distinguished for these higher levels also apply at the individual level. Also in other respects, such as the primary choice for a biocentric framework based on the inherent worth of animals, there is a close correspondence between the chapter about integrity and my own approach.

7. Conclusions

I started by referring to the moral and biological connotations of the central concepts which play such a dominant role in this part of the book: naturality, species-specificity, autonomy and integrity. Their moral connotation is derived from the concept of the intrinsic value (or inherent worth) of animals. In the biocentric approach this value is referring to the idea that animals have a good-of-their-own which ought te be respected by human beings. Three levels were distinguished on which this 'good' is manifested: the level of animality (autonomy), the level of species-specificity (naturality), and the level of the individual animal (integrity). Although the wild animal is the paradigmatic case to get to know this good for its own sake, one cannot say that domestic animals do not have a good of their own. Rather than saying that they are not natural, not independent I would say that they also have a 'nature' , that they are more or less independent, and we can surely speak about their integrity. In the form of a diagram we get:

intrinsic value as an non-gradual category, defining moral relevance

---

can be made operational at three levels of having a good of its own:

- level of *animality*: morally relevant criterion of *autonomy* (= self-activity)
- level of *species-specificity:* morally relevant criterion of *naturality* [besides autonomy]
- level of *individuality*: morally relevant criterion of *integrity* [besides autonomy and naturality]

We have seen in this contribution that the values at stake are not in any logical way 'derived' from facts about the animals; the ought is not derived from the is. It can not be proven why we *should* include animals into the moral domain, neither can we prove that humans should be included. But once we do so, animals automatically have to be respected because they have a good of their own. This step being taken we *have to* look into the animal's nature, we have to find out what is characteristic, what is essential. And here the biologist may come in to tell us more about the needs etc. of the animals involved. We must recognize, however, that 'the' biologist does not exist. This is exemplified in the chapter by Van den Bos, especially in his discussion with Wemelsfelder.

Biologists may be working at different levels of organization (from the behavioural to the molecular-biological), and more or less close to our daily (common sense) level of experience. And Wemelsfelder mentions people who keep or train animals, and who may not be scientists, with a sometimes impressive knowledge of the nature of animals. They talk about animals as subjects, with whom we can communicate in a second-person perspective (partners). It may well be that their knowledge is as important and as reliable as the often more detailed and reductionistic knowledge of biologists. Facts may not only come from scientists. There is even a curious paradox involved here. It may well be that the more value-free scientific knowledge is (in the sense of fully controllable and predictable under laboratory conditions: the standard meaning of objectivity), the less useful it may be for our moral judgement about how we ought to live with animals in a way which respects their good. For the latter we need knowledge which is objective in a different sense, namely corresponding with the real (what is essential). To use the words of Kass (1988), for that we need a more 'natural' science. In his Preface he says: "Our (scientific) knowledge of nature does not reach to its human import, to questions of meaning and goodness. This gap between nature studied scientifically and life lived naturally opens directly and necessarily because of the deliberate choice of modern science for "objectivity", for a stance outside of and removed from the world of our experience, from the world as it presents itself to us and as we engage it." (xi).

Especially when we are dealing with concepts which are close to our world of everyday life it is difficult to totally abstract from this world of common sense. It is not surprising, therefore, that concepts such as 'animal well-being' can best be called normative concepts. This view is defended by Tannenbaum (1991).

Tannenbaum rejects the 'pure-science-model', in which animal welfare is supposed to be a state of being of the animal, which can be described objectively. Tannenbaum argues that it is impossible to avoid value judgements in the choice of animals studied, in the choice of the level of animal welfare (minimal or optimal), in the definition of animal welfare, etc. Before the research starts fundamental normative choices have an influence on the kind of research done. It makes a great difference whether one defines 'animal welfare' as absence of suffering or as the animal's ability to perform its species-specific behaviour. Tannenbaum concludes that animal welfare science is (or ought to be) as much ethics as science. The difference between this approach to the relation between science and ethics, and the one put forward by Van den Bos needs further study. To do this here would go beyond the scope of this contribution.[3]

Acknowledgements

[3] This study has been made possible thanks to a grant of the Dutch Foundation of Scientific Research NWO (Program 'Ethiek & Beleid')

Notes

[1] This agrees with the formulation by Van den Bos (this volume): 'the concept of intrinsic value should be defined merely as opposed to and in direct relationship with the concept of instrumental value'.
[2] See Van den Bos where he compares his approach with the one of Wemelsfelder.

Literature

- Bartussek, H. (1991). A concept to define naturalness in animal production, in E. Boehncke &
- V.Molkenthin (Eds), *Proceedings of the International Conference on Alternatives in Animal Husbandry*, (pp. 309-319). Witzenhausen: Agrar Kultur Verlag.
- Bekoff, M. (1994). Cognitive ethology and the treatment of non-human animals: how matters of mind inform matters of welfare. *Animal Welfare*, 3, 75-96.
- Frankena, W.K. (1963). *Ethics*. Englewood Cliffs: Prentice Hall.
- Frankena, W.K. (1979). Ethics and the environment, in K.E. Goodpaster & K.M. Sayre (Eds), *Ethics and the problems of the 21st. century* , (pp. 3-20). Notre Dame/London: Univ. of Notre Dame Press.
- S. Kasanmoentalib (1994) De intrinsieke waarde van de natuur: wat kan de biologie daaraan bijdragen? *Filosofie & Paktijk*, 15 (3), 130-142.
- Kass, Leon R. (1988). *Towards a more natural science. Biology and human affairs*. New York: The Free Press.
- O'Neill, J. (1992). The varieties of intrinsic value. *The Monist* ,75, 119-137.
- Regan, T. (1984). *The case for animal rights*. London: Routledge & Kegan Paul.
- Rollin, B.E. (1981). *Animal rights and human morality*. New York: Prometheus Books.
- Singer , P. (1975). *Animal liberation*. New York: The New York Review.
- Tannenbaum J. (1991). Ethics and animal welfare: the inextricable connectio. *Journal of the American Vet erinary Medical Asssociation* , 198, 1360-1376.
- Taylor, P.W. (1984). Are humans superior to animals and plants? *Environmental ethics*, 6, 149-160.
- Taylor, P.W. (1986). *Respect for nature. A theory of environmental ethics*. Princeton: Princeton University Press.
- Verhoog, H. (1992). The concept of intrinsic value and transgenic animals. *Journal of Agricultural and Environmental Ethics*, 5/2, 147-160.
- Verhoog, H. (1997). Intrinsic value and animal welfare, in L.F.M. van Zutphen & M. Balls (Eds), *Animal alternatives, welfare and ethics*, (pp. 169-177). Amsterdam: Elsevier.
- Verhoog Henk & Visser Thijs (1997). A view of intrinsic value not based on animal consciousness, in Marcel Dol et al. (Eds), *Animal consciousness and animal ethics*, (pp. 223-232). Assen: Van Gorcum.
- Visser, Thijs & Verhoog, Henk (1986). De eigenwaarde van dieren en het dierenrecht. *Filosofie & Praktijk*, 7/3, 113-131.
- Wemelsfelder, Françoise (1997). Investigating the animal's point of view. An inquiry into a subject-based method of measurement in the field of animal welfare, in Marcel Dol et al (Eds), *Animal consciousness and animal ethics*, 73-89. Assen: Van Gorcum.

Part III

Intrinsic Value:
the Philosophical Issues

7

Intrinsic Value or Intrinsic Valuing?[1]

Albert W. Musschenga

1. Introduction

As every other species, humans have to extract from their natural environment the resources they need for their living. In contradistinction to other species, they lack the adaptation to a specific ecological niche. Therefore they have to change their environment to make it hospitable for them. In this process of interaction with his natural environment man creates culture. In creating culture he also develops himself. His needs become more refined and multiply in number. They seem to be unlimited. To satisfy these needs humans exploit increasing amounts of natural resources, such as water, land, plants, and animals. Not only do they consume natural resources and use them as raw material for the production of their artefacts, they also indirectly destroy or at least threaten the living conditions of plants, animals, entire species and ecosystems. The forests they chop down, and the land they cultivate used to be the habitat of many species of plants and animals. By polluting air and water they also affect the living conditions of plants and animals.

Over the last decades there is a growing insight that man has to regulate his interactions with his natural environment in order to prevent the destruction of the living conditions for himself, or at least for future human generations. Enlightened self-interest should motivate him to become more conscious of the indirect and long-term effects of his interactions with nature. But for many humans self-interest is not the only reason to worry about the fate of their fellow natural entities. For them it is not enough that humans start to care about natural entities because and insofar as the well-being of existing or future human generations is at stake. In their view the value of natural entities is not exhausted by their usefulness to human needs and goals. They question the alleged self-evidential superiority of humans which justifies their unlimited use of natural entities as material for the satisfaction of their needs. These environmentalists do of course realise that men cannot stop extracting resources from their natural environment. Their point is that natural entities should become objects of moral concern. That implies that human interactions with their natural environment should be regulated, contained by moral principles. Man should no longer be free to dispose of nature as he wishes. His interventions in nature have to be morally justified.

But why should man not be at liberty to dispose of natural entities as he wishes? An answer to that question which becomes increasingly popular is: "Because they have intrinsic value!" Although there are still many who regard the idea of nature having intrinsic value ridiculous, others find that this notion captures a deep seated feeling they have about nature.

The notion of the intrinsic value of nature is for many the cornerstone of a non-anthropocentric conception of environmental ethics. In their view, recognising the intrinsic value of nature and rejecting anthropocentrism are two sides of the same coin. The statement that nature has intrinsic value has even become the credo of the environmentalist movement. What is considered to be at stake is not only formulating an adequate conception of nature. It is thought that granting intrinsic value to nature will make a huge practical difference for decisions regarding nature: the consequence would, according to J. Baird Callicott, be that the burden of proof is lifted from the shoulders of conservationists and shifted onto the shoulders of those who, intentionally or unintentionally, knowingly or inadvertently, destroy nature (Baird Callicott 1995, [19]). Many environmentalists also take for granted that intrinsic value is *objective*, because in a subjective conception anthropocentrism should again sneak in through the backdoor. If it is their desirability which confers value upon natural entities, as is the case in subjective value theories, how could one avoid anthropocentrism? Values should give direction to human desiring.

Not all environmental ethicists are convinced that an environmental ethic needs to be non-anthropocentric. They prefer an ethic founded on an enlightened anthropocentrism, either because they reject non-anthropocentrism on normative grounds or because they have doubts about the motivational force of a non-anthropocentric ethic. Those who assert that nature has intrinsic value consider the range of such an ethic to be too limited. They find that an environmental ethic should be able to provide reasons for protecting even those natural entities that will probably never be of any interest for humans. In this article, I take sides with them. I grant that the idea of nature having intrinsic value is indispensable for a non-anthropocentric environmental ethic. Before I enter the field of environmental ethic, I will give a cartography of different conceptions of intrinsic value and their opposites.

2. Value for itself and in itself[2]

What is denied by affirming that nature has intrinsic value? The usual answer is: that nature has only instrumental value; that its value is determined by its usefulness for human purposes. In that answer, the opposite to intrinsic value is instrumental value. As Christine Korsgaard remarks, the opposite of intrinsic value is extrinsic value, while the opposite of instrumental value is final value (Korsgaard 1996). An object having final value means that it has value *for itself*. An object has value for itself, when it is, or can be, valued for its own sake, and not for the good of something else. In other words, the good of a final value is not dependent on the good of something else. An object has instrumental value if it is valued, not for its own sake *but for the sake of something else* - another instrumental value or a final value. In terms more common in ordinary language: a final value is an end, while an instrumental value is a means. If wealth is valued because it gives power, wealth is an instrumental and not a final value.

An object has intrinsic value if it has value *in itself*. An object which has value in itself does not derive its value from another source than itself. Its value is not *extrinsic*. An analogy may help to illuminate this. If a mayor is during his absence replaced by one of his aldermen, the authority of this alderman is extrinsic. He does not act in virtue of his own powers. His temporary powers are derived from those of the mayor. In Korsgaard's view intrinsic value as the opposite of extrinsic value is independent a double sense. First, its goodness does not depend on to the good of something else and, second, its goodness does not depend on the attitudes of human valuers. In this view, intrinsic value is objective because of its independence from human attitudes. Thus, in Korsgaard's view intrinsic value and instrumental value should not be treated as correlatives, because they belong to different distinctions.[3]

I think that Korsgaard's distinction between value for itself (final value) and in itself (intrinsic value) is an important one. It is often unclear what is meant by the non-instrumental value of nature: value for itself or in itself. Some authors seem to prefer to speak of value in itself because that seems to be the stronger claim.

In my view the idea of a value in itself is linked to a Kantian ethical theory. In Kantian ethical theories we owe respect to humans (persons) because they have absolute worth, 'Würde' (*Grundlegung*, 434f.). Kant's arguments run as follows. Humans are free and autonomous beings who embody the moral law. They regard their existence as an end in itself. This is still a subjective principle of action. The principle becomes objective as soon as man realises that every other rational being values himself in the same way. As an objective end, a rational being should be regarded as having Würde, whether or not it is desired or contributes to someone's happiness. All other things are subjective ends. They have only extrinsic value, that is, value because they are valued by humans, either for their utility, or for emotional reasons. In Kant's view only rational beings who value themselves as ends have worth. Thus, only they have value in themselves. This notion of value in itself can only be relevant for environmental ethics if it can be shown, per analogiam, that also non-humans can have worth.

I will not follow Korsgaard in reserving the term 'intrinsic value' 'for value in itself' largely for pragmatic reasons. I will refer to value in itself as 'worth' or 'intrinsic worth'. I also do not agree with her claim that the only final value is value for itself, while everything which does not have final value, has instrumental value. Value for itself - which I will from now on refer to as 'intrinsic value' - need not be final value. This can be illustrated by the Aristotelian ethical theory in which health is an intrinsic value but not a final one. The final intrinsic value is eudaimonia. Health can be valued both for itself and as a component of eudaimonia. Unlike may ethicists I will not reject subjective conceptions of intrinsic value outright. Except for Baird Callicott, a subjective conception of the intrinsic value of nature is hardly taken seriously in environmental ethics for reasons already mentioned. In my opinion, that is regrettable. Environmental ethicists have to discuss the reasons why many mainstream moral philosophers reject the objectivity of value. Any serious environmental ethic based on the intrinsic value or worth of nature, has to explain how it deals with this criticism. This is the first task I want to take on in this article. The second task concerns the relation between the intrinsic value of nature or worth and moral duties regarding nature. The relation between the intrinsic value or worth of nature and duties regarding nature is not analytic. The role of these notions in grounding duties regarding nature depends on the type of ethical theory one adheres to. In the literature on environmental ethics we find three main types of ethical theories based on a recognition of nature having intrinsic value or worth: (i) a deontological theory based on an objective conception of intrinsic worth (ii) a teleological theory based on a subjective conception of intrinsic value and (iii) a teleological theory based on a objective conception of intrinsic value.

I discuss the three types of theories in the section 3-5. I will reject (i) as implausible. In the sections 6-7 I discuss subjective and objective value theories. The discussion will be concluded with an outline of a teleological environmental ethic based on a modified objective theory of the intrinsic value of nature. In the final sections 8-10 I refine this theory and discuss its non-anthropocentric quality.

3. Respect for nature

At first sight the environmental ethic of Paul Taylor seems to be modelled on the basis of a Kantian conception of intrinsic worth. Taylor makes distinction between what he calls 'inherent worth' and intrinsic value (Taylor 1986).[4] What makes living beings worthy of respect is according to him not having moral autonomy, but having a good of their own. What does he mean by 'having a good of their own'? "Some entities in the universe are such that we can meaningfully speak of their having a good of their own, while other entities are of a kind that makes such a judgement nonsense" (1986, 60). "They have a good of its own because it makes sense to speak of their being benefited or harmed. Things that happen to them can be judged to be favourable or unfavourable to them" (63). Which entities have a good of their own? An entity has a good of their own if we can speak of what is good or bad *for* the thing in question, without reference to any other entity (61). Such entities are individual organisms as well as species populations and ecosystems.

Taylor makes a sharp distinction between the is-statement that a being has a good of its own, and the ought-statement that agents have a duty to promote or protect its good or refrain from harming it. How does Taylor bridge that gap? His argument runs as follows. Any valid system of human ethics has to embody the principle of respect for all persons as persons. Persons are beings that consciously aim at ends or take means to achieve such ends. They have interests in achieving these ends. To harm or to benefit human beings means to frustrate or further their interests. The human good can be defined in terms of the interest they have (or should have if they were fully rational, autonomous and enlightened beings). Although animals and plants do not have interests, this difference is not morally relevant. The morally relevant similarity between them and human beings is having a good of their own. Animals and plants may not *have interests* because they do not consciously aim at ends, but everything that contributes to their own good can be said to be *of interest* for them. Therefore, if respect is the moral attitude human beings should have to persons as persons, they should also have respect for animals and plants. If they do, they will conceive of them as possessing inherent worth. Inherent worth is the fundamental value-presupposition of the attitude of respect.

Taylor's argument is very sophisticated. He explicitly states that one may recognise an entity as having a good of its own, while at the same time *not* regard it as possessing inherent worth. Only if one adopts a biocentric outlook on nature in which human beings are not seen as superior entities, and if one regards the attitude of respect to be central to ethics, then one will conceive of not only human beings but also animals and plants as having inherent worth.

Taylor's concept of inherent worth is parasitic on Kant's concept of worth. What he means by it is value which is independent from an object's usefulness for, and being valued by conscious beings. For Kant only beings which can value their existence as end in itself can be said to have worth. Only they do not derive their value from another source than themselves. Taylor's concept of inherent worth boils down to an objective concept of value for itself - of what I call 'intrinsic value'.

In an important respect Taylor is still a Kantian. For Kant all rational and autonomous beings have equal worth. Likewise for Taylor all living organisms as teleological life centres are equal in having inherent worth. Here he is in complete agreement with Tom Regan who says: "Inherent value (i.e. value in itself in my terminology, awm) is thus a categorical concept ... It does not come in degrees" (Regan 1983, 240f.) The same egalitarianism in present in Taylor's views. He of course recognises that beings differ in capacities from other living things. He argues that not their capacities as such serve as the ground of their inherent worth. It is the way in which these are organised. They are interrelated functionally so that the organism as a whole can be said to be a teleological life centre. That is, it is something which has a good of its own which it seeks to realise (Taylor, ch. 3).

It is of course easy to criticise Taylor from a point of view far outside his ethical theory and his biocentric view on nature. I will argue that the implications of his egalitarianism are counterintuitive also for those who do not regard humans to be self-evidently superior to other living beings. These implications lead us to reconsider the soundness of the idea of living beings having equal intrinsic value or worth.

As a consequence of his egalitarian view, Taylor has to find principles for the resolution of conflicts between the interests between humans and non-humans which are species-impartial in not assigning greater inherent worth to humans. I will not spell out Taylor's ingenious system of priority principles in detail. Central in that system is the distinction between basic and non-basic interests. Basic interests are those whose fulfilment is needed by an organism if it is to remain alive (271). In the case of humans, basic interests are what rational and factually enlightened people would value as an essential part of their very existence as persons (272). All other interests are non-basic. Non-basic interests of one species are not allowed to override basic interests of another species. What if human beings are attacked by, say, a lion who is starving for lack of food? We then have a conflict of basic interests. In such cases, humans have the right to defend themselves.

In many cases Taylor's priority principles lead to plausible solutions of conflicts between interests. But there are cases in which the outcome raises doubts about the soundness of his idea of all living beings having equal inherent worth. For Taylor there is no morally relevant difference between eating meat or eating plants, if the animals are killed painlessly. Humans are justified in killing for food all kinds of animals, provided that the survival of a species- population is not threatened. They are then free to choose between, say, pig, chicken, chimp, bonobo, and so on. In my view, this is counterintuitive. We would blame someone for killing a bonobo for food, if there were other animals such as chickens available. I do not believe that this intuition will disappear in critical reasoning. I am also not sure whether in Taylor's view it would be justified to destroy a very rare virus which is affecting the health of a population of, say, chimpanzees, though not seriously.

Taylor's egalitarianism thus has, in my view, counterintuitive implications. This observation calls for a closer look at the foundations of his ideas about intrinsic worth. He claims that within a biocentric outlook, all teleological life centres deserve the same equal respect and concern which, in Kant's view, is only bestowed on persons. The personhood of human beings does not endow them with a greater inherent worth. For all living things the opportunity to pursue their good is of equal importance. The fact that humans as persons strive for consciously chosen ends makes no difference. Taylor does not make the mistake of placing the self-organisation of organisms on a par with moral autonomy. He does not argue that we should respect organisms as we do persons, because there are relevant similarities between moral autonomy and the self-organisation of other organisms. The relevant similarity lies on a more basic level. It is the property of having a good of their own. Moral autonomy is only a special kind of the capacity of self-organisation which all organisms possess.

Some authors have tried to develop a deontological theory of environmental ethics which does not run into the difficulties associated with Taylor's view. They argue that the principle of respect for living entities does not presuppose them having equal worth. In this reasoning organisms have a worth that is *similar*, but not *identical* to human worth (e.g. Brom 1998, 111). This view can be interpreted in two ways. First, it can mean that the conception of worth has to be related to the specific nature of a species and its good. This reading stays within the framework of Taylor's theory. He speaks of the worth of diverse organisms being equal, not identical. Second it can mean that organisms can vary in degree of worth. In my view this last interpretation is not compatible with the central stake of deontological environmental ethics. The basic assumption of such a theory is that moral membership should be assigned to all living entities - or at least to a broader range of species than that of humans. Moral membership implies having the right to be treated equally. The sole difference between humans and other members of the moral community is that only humans can have moral duties. Human duties to other living beings are correlative to the rights of these beings. If one drops the idea of equal moral worth, that results in a collapse of the basis under a deontological environmental ethic in which the interests of non-humans are morally relevant because they are members of the moral community.

If my argument above is valid, we have to conclude that one cannot found environmental ethics on the concept of intrinsic worth. As I shall show in section 10, this has consequences for the possibility of formulating a strong non-anthropocentric ethic. So we are left with two non-moral conceptions of intrinsic value, the subjective and the objective one.

4. Values without valuers?

The objective conception of intrinsic value is usually associated with G.E. Moore. In Moore's theory, intrinsic value refers to the value an object has solely in virtue of its intrinsic properties. The intrinsic properties of an object are indefinable, i.e. simple and unanalysable, non-natural qualities. The test of intrinsic value proceeds by considering if objects keep their value "if they existed *by themselves*, in absolute isolation" (Moore 1903, 187). Intrinsic value is for Moore non-relational in three senses: it is not related to (i) the good of something else, (ii) the valuings of valuers and, (iii) the existence or non-existence of other objects. The third sense of 'non-relational' implies that properties such as rarity cannot confer intrinsic value upon an object, since objects can only be rare within a particular context, related to the (non-)existence of other objects.

Moore mentions love and beauty as examples of intrinsic value. Noam Lemos, whose conception of objective intrinsic value belongs to the same family of value theories, does mention nature as a bearer of intrinsic value (Lemos 1994, xx). In this tradition, intrinsic value is not equal. Bearers of intrinsic value can differ as to the quantity of intrinsic value. Besides that, one has to distinguish between the rank of intrinsic values. Some values are higher than others. Lemos speaks here of 'the principle of rank'. Relevant for our subject is also Moore's 'principle of organic unity' which says that the value of a whole need not be the same as the sum of the values of its parts. Although Moore's concept of organic unity should not be confused with the biological concept of the same name, the principle can, in my view, be applied to biological entities such as ecosystems. It might then be argued that an ecosystem has greater or smaller intrinsic value than the sum of its parts. When applying the principle of rank, one might also conclude that the value of an ecosystem is higher or lower than that of its parts.

What is, in Moore's view, the relation between intrinsic value and moral obligation? William K. Frankena interprets Moore as asserting that we have a prima facie obligation to promote what is intrinsically good (Frankena 1942). In others words, it follows from the nature of intrinsic goodness that it ought to be promoted. The connection between intrinsic value and obligation is an analytic one. Frankena argues that to define intrinsic value wholly or partially in terms of the notion that certain agents have a duty to do a certain thing, implies asserting that it is complex and relational. Intrinsic goodness can have a normative character only if it essentially or analytically involves a reference to an agent on whom something is actually or hypothetically enjoined. Intrinsic value is then defined in terms of obligation. In that case, it is not a simple, undefinable intrinsic quality. If goodness is either simple or a quality, it can be connected with obligation only synthetically (Frankena, 99). The reason for thinking that any ethical notion is essentially undefinable is its apparent normative character. Therefore, if intrinsic value is an intrinsic quality or if its connection with obligation is only synthetic, then there is no reason to regard it as essentially irreducible to non-ethical terms (103).

I conclude that Moore did not succeed in showing that intrinsic value possess any essential normativeness or obligatoriness. The relation between intrinsic value and obligation is synthetic. An object having intrinsic value provides us with reasons for choosing and acting. However, it only makes sense to speak of an obligation or duty to objects having intrinsic value if one has accepted the perspective of an ethical theory which knows of a principle to do good or to prevent harm. If one has thus accepted that the connection between intrinsic value and obligation is synthetic, there is no reason to stick to the view that intrinsic value is non-relational in the third sense of not being related to the existence or non-existence of other objects. In that case it need no longer be an implication of the definition of intrinsic value to assume that objects keep their value "if they existed *by themselves*, in absolute isolation". The idea that there could be a world full of intrinsic value without there being valuing subjects conflicts with common sense. Intrinsically valuable objects are objects worthy of being desired for what they are. Talk of intrinsic values presupposes the presence of subjects who can come to recognise their desirability.

Let it be clear that the above criticism does not lead me to rejecting this theory of intrinsic value completely. Lemos's version of the theory contains many valuable elements. However, I did not mention the most problematic feature of such a value theory. It concerns the ontological status of objective values. I will come back to that issue in section 6.

5. Intrinsic value as instrinsic valuing

According to O'Neill (1992), environmental ethicists often think that intrinsic values can only be accounted for within an objectivist value theory. They assume that the intrinsic value of natural entities cannot be defended within a subjectivist value theory which holds that nothing can have value independent of its being valued by humans. In their view, environmental ethics based on a subjective value theory cannot overcome the evil of anthropocentrism. Although such a theory does not necessarily imply that non-humans have only instrumental value, the fate of non-human entities still depends on the contingent content of human valuings. Baird Callicott is among the few environmental ethicists who have come out as subjectivists in value theory. He suggests "... that we base our environmental ethics on our human capacity to value nonhuman natural entities for what they are - irrespective both of what they may do for us and of whether or not they can value themselves. And this we can do regardless of the nature of the object of our intentional act of intrinsic valuation as long as we think we have good reason to value it intrinsically" (Baird Callicott 1995, [67[).

In subjective value theories, the basic concept is that of valuation. A recent and important elaboration of a subjective theory is that of Gerald Gaus (1990). He speaks of 'valuing' instead of valuation. In Gaus's theory valuings are prior to value judgements. *Valuings* are dispositional emotions toward objects, *value judgements* concern the appropriateness of certain valuings, and *values* or 'a person's values' are either important and abstract valuings or patterns of valuings (10). What is the difference between valuing and value judgement? Contrary to valuings, value judgements do not presuppose a personal experience of an emotion. I can assert that, given the relevant impersonal criteria, a particular woman is beautiful. These may be the criteria of popular opinion, experts or authorities. However, I need not be personally attracted by that woman. In that case, my judgement is an *impersonal value judgement*. A *personal value judgement* asserts that X is valuable based on (i) apprehending X in the relevant affective mode and (ii) a conviction, or at least an assumption that this emotional response is appropriate (158,9).

Gaus makes a distinction between intrinsic and extrinsic valuings. An object that is valued intrinsically, is valued for its own sake. An object is valued extrinsically or instrumentally if it is valued for the sake of another valued object (130). The source of an instrumentally valued object is always extrinsic. Its value is derivative: All extrinsic valuings are grounded on intrinsic valuings. Intrinsic valuings are foundational, that is, they are not grounded on any other valuing (140). Gaus uses the notions of instrumental and extrinsic as equivalent. In his theory, the distinctions between intrinsic and extrinsic at the one side, and at the other side final and instrumental, coincide.

As any other objects natural entities can be valued intrinsically. The appropriateness of such valuing is stated in judgements about the intrinsic valuableness of natural entities. 'The intrinsic value of nature' then means something like 'a person's (or a group's) intrinsic valuings of nature'. A person's judgement that nature is intrinsically valuable does not imply that he himself actually values nature. His judgement may be impersonal. Since value judgements have to be analysed in terms of valuings, it makes no sense to state that nature has intrinsic value even if there were no human valuers.[5]

Environmental ethicists are especially interested in proving that nature has intrinsic value because they think it makes a difference for justifying duties regarding nature. In non-moral value theory intrinsic values constitute the good life. In teleological ethical theory it is a moral duty to promote the good. In a teleological theory of environmental ethics which is combined with a subjective value theory humans have a moral duty not to damage, to preserve and to protect natural entities if and only if they ascribe intrinsic value to them. Because they are relative to contingent human intrinsic valuations, such duties are relative, and not universal.

6. Intinsic value: subjective or objective

I suppose that many environmentalists would agree with Brian G. Norton who remarks: "Callicott has denied the objectivity of environmental values in any sense that would be helpful in environmental policy, because environmental values are the subjective judgments of those environmentalists" (Norton 1992, 221). In their view, it is the task of environmental ethics to provide everyone with reasons for not damaging, protecting and preserving natural entities, regardless whether they themselves value these entities instrumentally or intrinsically. If an ethic based on a subjective value theory cannot fulfil that task, that is in their view a sufficient reason to reject such a theory.

It goes without saying that we cannot simply choose the kind of value theory that lines up most with our normative ethical aspirations. We cannot just state that a value theory has to be objective. We will have to show that such a value theory is plausible and superior to a subjective one. In the meta-ethical discussion on the nature of values, two issues are at stake. Objectivists argue that the only plausible conception of value is one in which value is independent of human desires and provides everyone irrespective of their desires with reasons for action. If value is intimately linked to desire, it would only provide reasons to do what people are already motivated to do. Such a conception of value simply makes no sense. That is why values have to be objective. Subjectivists contend that the point of giving reasons is to influence human actions. Therefore, values as reasons for action must have some connection with human motivation. Both are serious issues which cannot be simply discarded. I will call these 'the problem of supra-subjective validity' and 'the problem of motivation'.

6.1. The truth of objective theories
Objectivists argue that their theory is supported by moral experience. "We *value* a thing to discover that we are under the sway of its *valence*", says Holmes Rolston III in an article about the subjectivity/objectivity of values in nature (Rolston 1982, 143). A theory in which values are represented as projections on a neutral world is not able to explain this experience. A similar position is taken by Charles Taylor:

(But) I think one can argue that there is a demand on us to respect the integrity of the wilderness areas, for example, which goes beyond the call of long-term prudence (which is urgent enough, to be sure). The demand has something to do with what we are as language beings on the one hand, and with the way we as language beings fit into and emerge from our world on the other. To understand what is involved here is to see that the 'Ding an sich'/transcendent reality distinction can get no purchase. The very idea of projectivism makes no sense. There is nothing further out there to project *on*.

I want to speak of this demand as something that we discover. And so I want to go on thinking of myself as a moral realist (...) (1991, 246).

Subjectivists need not deny this experience. In their view such an experience is similar to the observation that the sun disappears beyond the horizon or that the earth is flat. These beliefs are quite understandable but wrong. Of course, the falsity of objective value theories cannot be proven empirically. But in the view of subjectivists objectivists fail to give a plausible picture of values having an objective existence.

What does, according to objectivists, the objectivity of values consists in? The Platonic conception of values making up part of the fabric of the universe is rejected by almost every contemporary objectivist. The model that many of them use to represent the objectivity of values is that of secondary qualities. According to John Locke in his *An Essay Concerning Human Understanding*, secondary qualities are those whose instantiation in an object consists in a power or disposition of the object to produce sensory experiences of a certain phenomenological character in perceivers; whereas primary qualities are said not to consist in such dispositions to produce experiences (Locke 1964, passim; see also McGinn 1983, 5).[6] Secondary qualities are only adequately conceivable in terms of dispositions to give rise to certain subjective states. Thus, in a certain sense they are subjective. However, they are not subjective in the sense of being a mere product, a fiction of subjective states. In contrast to that, a primary quality can be adequately understood without reference to dispositions of giving rise to subjective states (McDowell 1985, 113). If values are conceived as secondary qualities, their being good is seen to consist in a propensity on the part of good things to elicit in observers reactions of moral approval. Any account of what it is for an object to have a moral property will have to make essential reference to certain psychological reactions in appropriately constituted beings (McGinn 147). The analogy between colours and values is that neither of them is brutely 'there'. Although they exist independently of our experience of them, they are not independent of our sensibility.

John Mackie is undoubtedly the most vehement contemporary critic of value objectivism. For him, the idea of values having an objective existence, is queer. Values are not objective. They are projected on the world by humans. Mackie recognises that objectivism about values is not only a feature of the philosophical tradition, but has also a firm basis in ordinary thought. Ordinary moral judgements include a claim to objectivity. But we should realise that it is false. The phenomenology of value needs to be corrected by a non-cognitivist theory (Mackie 1977, 30ff.). Mackie's argument for rejecting the objectivity of values is that, according to that view, value-entities should have a property which makes them different from all other entities we know. They should have the property to influence the will without being connected to a desire or an interest. In such a view, the knowledge of a value-entity provides the knower with both a direction for his actions and an overriding reason and motive to act in that direction. We have to postulate a faculty which 'sees' not only the natural properties which make that an object can be said to carry a certain value, but also its 'to-be-pursuedness' which is built into it, and the relation between the natural properties and that of 'to-be-pursuedness' (Mackie 1977, 38ff.).

According to Mackie value judgements cannot be represented as perceptions. His model of perception is that of awareness of primary qualities. Secondary-quality perception, as conceived by a pre-philosophical consciousness, involves a projective error analogous to the one he discovers in evaluative thought. If values are objective, they should be represented as primary qualities. Such a representation confronts us with the above mentioned difficulties. If Mackie is right in his view on secondary qualities, there is indeed no plausible ground for value objectivism. For Mackie, there is no difference between a colour and a shape figuring in experience. All properties of objects are phenomenal, intelligible in terms of how these objects are disposed to appear to perceiving subjects. In both cases the intrinsic features of experience function as vehicles for particular aspects of their representational content. To experience an object as red and as, say, square, is to attribute a property to that object.

McDowell counters that, in Mackie's view, one loses hold of Locke's intuition that primary qualities are distinctive in being both objective and perceptible. Primary qualities are not phenomenal the way secondary qualities are. He states that we have to reject the idea that intrinsic features of experience function as vehicles for particular aspects of their representational content. Colours and shapes figure in experience simply as properties that objects are represented as having.

These properties are distinctively phenomenal in the one case (secondary qualities) and not so in the other (primary qualities). We will not achieve a satisfactory understanding of experience without taking experience's radical subjectivity into account (McDowell 115ff.). To be red simply is to be the sort of thing that looks red or would look red to normal human observers in the perceptual circumstances that normally obtain in the world. While to be square is an independent property which can be used to explain many things about an object, including how it looks and feels.

I am inclined to follow McGinn and McDowell in their defence of the concept of secondary qualities. But it falls outside the scope of this article to provide knockdown arguments for this position. What should interest us here is whether the analogy between secondary qualities and values is plausible. A serious objection is that the notion of moral error becomes problematic. It is suggested that within this analogy moral error pairs off with colour-blindness. Due to a deficiency in their perceptual apparatus, colour-blind people are unable to make certain discriminations. McGinn objects that those who are morally wrong about a certain case need not have lesser capacities in discriminating morally relevant features. They rather assign the wrong value to a situation (152).[7]

It is evident that the capacity of value judgement differs from psychophysiological sensory capacities. To be able to judge correctly, a being needs, besides sensitivity and imagination, capacities of reasoning, an adequate framework of concepts, and a good character. The analogy between the knowledge of secondary qualities and that of value will only becoming convincing if it is supplemented by a plausible theory of the moral subject.

This insight is, at least *in nuce*, present in McDowell's views. He recognises that experience of something as valuable is conceived to be not merely such as to elicit the appropriate attitude, but rather such as to *merit* it (McDowell, 118). McDowell elaborates this point in connection with something that is not a value, namely danger or the fearful. To experience something as fearful cannot be explained satisfyingly as a projection. We make sense of fear by seeing it as a response to objects that *merit* such a response. The claim that reality contains nothing in the way of fearfulness would undermine the intelligibility that the explanations confer on our responses (McDowell, 199). We can of course always discuss whether someone is right in saying that an object is fearful. We do so because we are prepared to attribute to at least some possible objects of fear, the properties that would validate these responses. The same applies to value experiences. Value experiences are always contentious. No sensible person would think that his evaluative outlook is incapable of improvement. But that need not stop him from supposing that the objects of at least some of his value experiences do merit his responses (McDowell, 120).

While Mackie explains how we have come to believe in the objectivity of values, Taylor explains how many people have come to believe that objective theories are implausible. A subjective value theory fits into a modern conception of identity, the conception of a 'detached', 'disengaged' self that is free to reject all claims coming from the outside as alien to his identity. According to Taylor ecology and evolutionary biology confront us with the fact that man is part of, and evolved out of, natural reality. That is what he means when speaking of the way we as language beings fit into and emerge from our world'. A similar view is defended by Holmes Rolston III. Humans as valuers of nature are themselves part of nature. The valuing subject is itself a natural product. Rolston refers to Dewey who says that experience is *in* as well as *of* nature (Rolston 1982, 135).[8]

Mackie does not deal with questions about the value of nature. His theory of morality only regards those human actions which impinge on the interests and well-being of others. That is precisely the part of human morality for which a contract theoretical perspective might give a plausible account of the authority of moral judgements. Such a perspective is irrelevant when discussing the grounds for e.g. judgements about the value of nature.

Objective value theories need not be queer. But can they deal with the problem of motivation? I will not review the diverse accounts of the connection between value judgements and motivation which are given by objective theories. What interests me is whether a plausible account can be given from the perspective of such theories. The most familiar one is that of Thomas Nagel which he first developed in his *The Possibility of Altruism* (1970). He argues that not only desires, but also reasons are capable of motivating. The judgement that one has reason to do something includes the acceptance of a justification for doing it, and that is its motivational content (65). An interesting account from a Humean perspective is given by E.J. Bond. He argues that the judgement that something is valuable produces a desire for it. The justifying reason and the motivating reason then become one and the same reason (Bond 1983, 57). I regard Nagel's and Bond's views as complementary.

6.2. The truth of subjective theory

Gaus rejects all claims that values are objective.[9] To do justice to Gaus's position, it is important to recall his distinction between personal and impersonal value judgements. Contrary to valuings, value judgements do not presuppose a personal experience of an emotion. I can assert that *X* is, given the relevant impersonal criteria, valuable. These may be the criteria of popular opinion, experts or authorities. However, I need not value that object myself. If that is the case, my judgement is an *impersonal value judgement*. A *personal value judgement* asserts that *X* is valuable based on (i) apprehending *X* in the relevant affective mode and (ii) a conviction, or at least an assumption that this emotional response is appropriate (158,9). I can judge something to be valuable which I myself do not actually value, but which is valued by others. Such an impersonal value judgement might have some motivational force for me. This force might be strengthened by a belief that I may come to value that object in a certain situation or in a certain stage of my life.

In my view, to claim objectivity for value judgements is an indispensable property of value talk. This is an important argument for preferring an objective theory. As I argued in the previous section, the objectivity of values is not queer. Bond's theory offers a useful step towards a solution for the problem of motivation. However, a subjective theory such as that of Gaus has also some strong points which should and need not be discarded. Objective theories focus on value judgements, while Gaus regards valuings as basic. They are indeed basic, but not in the way Gaus suggests. It is an observational fact that many people do value nature intrinsically. The experience of such a positive emotional disposition moves them to reflect on the value of nature. Thus, valuings are basic from a phenomenological point of view. This can also be recognised within an objective theory. Lemos states that there is a strong tradition of objective value theory that takes emotional experience as a source or warrant for beliefs about values. Other theories hold that value can be known by emotional experience (Lemos 1994, 180 f.).

The order of knowing is not necessarily from valuings to value judgement. A belief in the intrinsic value of natural entities moves me to find out whether I myself can also value these entities intrinsically. In valuing intrinsically what I already judged to be intrinsically valuable, I develop a positive emotional disposition toward these entities. The desire for these entities arises in the course of my quest for them; a quest which is motivated by my belief in their valuableness. However, I cannot be said to desire them because they are valuable. My desiring and valuing them confirms my knowing that they are valuable.

Another strong point in Gaus's theory is his view on personal value judgements. Usually personal value judgements are conceived as judgements on the basis of criteria which are endorsed by the agent. Criteria used in impersonal value judgements are then derived from an authority - e.g. a person or a tradition. In Gaus's view, a value judgement about an object, e.g. a natural entity, can only be personal if the agent himself experiences a positive emotional disposition. In this view, personal judgements have an affective dimension which impersonal ones are lacking. They presuppose a valuing. Although impersonal value judgements do have some implications for action, these implications cannot be as strong as those of actual valuings. The reason is that there are simply more things worthy of being valued than I can possibly value. When deliberating about action, my focus will be on the things I actually value.

Gaus's view does justice to the affective relation between a person and his personal values. I think he is also right in arguing that the motivational force of personal value judgements is stronger than that of impersonal ones. Personal value judgements not only have the motivational force of justifying reasons for action, they are also affectively supported by valuings. In contradistinction to that, impersonal value judgements only have the motivational force of the reasons which justify them.

What is missing in Gaus's account is the possibility that a person endorses values with which he has no affective relations. I do regard more objects as valuable than I value. This can be accounted for within a pluralistic value theory. On the basis of such a theory one may distinguish between conceptions of the good and life-plans. I can come to recognise many, sometimes incompatible and incommensurable, values. Together they constitute my conception of the good. However, there are obviously limits to the amount of values which I can incorporate in my life-plan. The reasons are, first, that some of these value are incompatible, and, second, that my skills and talents, my knowledge and sensitivities are too limited to experience and realise all of them. I will therefore value only a part of those objects which I judge to be valuable. These values form the normative core of my life-plan. I will always be more motivated by reasons provided by personal value judgements than by impersonal ones.

Environmentalists who are objectivists in value theory accuse, as we have seen, subjectivists such as Baird Callicott of holding that environmental values are but the subjective judgments of environmentalists, who are already convinced that we need an ecological ethic. They are right insofar as they point to the lack of objectivity in such an account of environmental values. But it is naive to suppose that it should make no difference whether one is a nature lover or not. Nature lovers are persons for whom the intrinsic value of natural entities is part of the normative core of their life-plan. It is often not sufficient to confront people with objectively valid reasons for preserving natural entities. Even if they accept these reasons as binding upon them and are rationally motivated by them, it is still possible that these reasons are outweighed by other ones. To gain motivational force, these rational motivations need to be supplemented by the positive emotional dispositions of personal valuings. To be effective, an environmental movement needs a large core of people who are doubly motivated.

Before going on I will recapitulate my findings and conclusions. I rejected Paul Taylor's deontological theory of environmental ethics because (i) it must be doubted that his notion of inherent worth is really different from objective value for itself and (ii) his idea of the equality of inherent worth is implausible. I then analysed Moore's objective conception of value. I concluded that we have to reject (i) Moore's view on the analytical relation between intrinsic value and moral obligation and (ii) his idea that intrinsic value is non-relational. I underlined that there are many valuable elements in the tradition of thinking about intrinsic value in which Moore stands, which recur in the modern version developed by Noam Lemos. I then turned to the subjective conception of intrinsic value which is largely (but not wholly) absent in environmental ethics. I summarised Gaus's subjective value theory which in my view could offer a framework for a more sophisticated elaboration of subjective conceptions of the intrinsic value of nature. After discussing - in section 6 - the strengths and weaknesses of subjective and objective theories of value, I developed what one could call 'a modified objective value theory' that tries to supplement objective theories with an account of intrinsic valuation. However, I still have to make clear what kind of obligations regarding nature result from the combination of this modified objective value theory and a teleological ethical theory. I deal with that in section 7. In sections 8 and 9 I refine my theory, first, by introducing a distinction between intrinsic value and its constituents and, second, by developing a non-egalitarian account of intrinsic value. In section 10 I will end with briefly discussing to which extent my theory is (non-)anthropocentric.

7. Intrinsic value, the good life, and duties regarding nature

In deontological theories humans have a moral duty to respect natural entities because these have worth. According to Paul Taylor we have such a duty to all entities that have a good of their own. Such duties function as side-constraints to actions of humans which are directed to their own good. What grounds the moral concern for the fate of natural entities in my account? In teleological theories, the most fundamental moral obligation is to do good and prevent harm. This principle also applies to natural entities bearing intrinsic value. Actions which harm natural entities and diminish their intrinsic value are prima facie wrong. What is usually wrong with our dealings with animals and other natural entities is that they are based on deficiencies in understanding and recognising their intrinsic value.

We have to (re)discover the intrinsic value of natural entities so that their fate will get a place in our moral deliberations. Affect-laden experiences, valuings of natural entities are an important entry to the knowledge of their intrinsic value. Many environmental ethicists have pointed to the central role of perceptions and images for our dealings with nature (Achterberg 1994). They rightly argue that a change in behaviour requires much more than new moral principles. My theory does justice to this central role of perceptions and images - more so, I think, than a deontological theory focused on a cognitive-rational recognition of the worth of entities. What is needed above all is a change in our perceptions, our images of natural entities, and not in the least in our images of the relation between humans and other natural entities.

It is well known from concentration camps that due to the conditions of living, the behaviour of prisoners tends to reflect their loss of self-respect and dignity. If they also stop attending to their physical appearance and become dirty, this will strengthen their oppressors in believing that the prisoners are inferior beings. Something similar may happen to animals held in captivity, or animals such as chickens, pigs, and calves which are fattened in very small and sometimes dark pens. They lose almost all the intrinsic value they might display under more favourable conditions. They are bereaved of their potentialities to bear intrinsic value. This is prima facie morally wrong. The dominance of instrumental attitudes towards natural entities hinders us in discovering and perceiving their full intrinsic value.

I have argued that natural entities as bearers of intrinsic values should get a place in our conception of the good, of what is intrinsically valuable in the world. But I added that there are no objective reasons for individuals to prefer intrinsically valuable natural entities over other entities that also have considerable intrinsic value. Although everyone has a prima facie duty not to harm the interests of natural entities bearing intrinsic value, there is no general duty to promote the good of these entities. Individuals need to, and are justified to make a selection out of the pool of values and valuable entities. Enjoying the intrinsic values of natural entities may be central to the life plan of some, but not to that of others. Those for whom these values are central, will agree with Arne Naess who says that experiencing the intrinsic value of nature contributes to the 'quality of life' (Naess 1989, passim). Environmental education and personal experiences with natural entities are indispensable for setting people on the trail of the intrinsic value of natural entities. People will have to discover for themselves what the intrinsic value of natural entities is. That is why environmental policies that close large areas to all human visitors might in the long run turn out to be counterproductive. People should be able to experience from time to time the intrinsic value of those areas and entities which are protected by such policies.

An interesting question is whether in this account it still makes sense to speak of respect for nature - which is the fundamental principle in Paul Taylor's theory. In his theory the respect that humans can acquire for nature grounds their duties to nature. Humans are prima facie obliged to natural entities not to frustrate the good they have of their own. If they do, humans do not only harm, they also *wrong* them.

In my theory humans have moral duties concerning natural entities because and insofar as they have intrinsic value. These are not duties *towards* natural entities, but *concerning* these entities as bearers of intrinsic value. However, it still makes sense to speak of respect for natural entities. But the notion of respect has changed. It is no longer respect for living entities as members of the moral community. One can, e.g., speak of a duty to respect the integrity of, say, the Notre Dame in Paris or the 'Nachtwacht' of the Dutch painter Rembrandt. The basis for such respect is not a moral, but non-moral notion of intrinsic value. The Notre Dame and the 'Nachtwacht' exemplify important intrinsic values. In moral persons full recognition of the intrinsic value of natural entities will lead to respecting them. A moral person is then someone who has learned what is intrinsically valuable, what are the components of a truly good and happy life. This notion of respect is different from the Kantian one, which is based on recognition of worth.

I will end this section by conceding that the two types of ethical theories I discussed - the deontological and the teleological - do not exhaust the whole range of ethical theories. There is also the mixed teleological-deontological theory which is defended by e.g. William K. Frankena. It falls beyond the scope of this article to examine whether my modified theory of objective intrinsic value can be combined with such a mixed theory. I think it can, but I will not argue for that. In this article I take issie with pure deontological theories only.

8. Value constituents and the intrinsic value of nature and animals

Environmental ethicists often just state that nature has intrinsic value, without a further explanation. From the perspective of a deontological theory that is all one needs to know. In such a theory, all entities having intrinsic worth are qualified for moral membership. Within a teleological theory one has to know what makes something valuable for its own sake. In many theories, intrinsic value is conceptually primitive, that is, it cannot be explained in terms of other values. A different view is defended by Warren Quinn. He states that a property is good-making, first, with respect to particulars of a specific kind and, second, with respect to a specific type of value. His example is honesty as good-making with respect to persons as particulars and moral worth as values. The good-making property is *constitutive* of whatever value belongs to the objects which possess it. Hence it is constitutive of the goodness of the objects which possess it (1974, 126f.). I call such a good-making property a 'value constituent'. An intrinsic value constituent is a standard for assessing the intrinsic value of an object. Objects may have one or more intrinsic value constituents

The advantage of this conception of intrinsic value is that it always makes sense to ask what an object's intrinsic value consists of. Those who contend that something has intrinsic value will have to explicate what its value constituents are. Let me give an example. Imagine a tree growing on a strangely humid place in an arid area. It is the only one in the entire area. Rarity is one of its value constituents. Besides that, the crown of the tree is full and balanced. The tree is also big and impressive. By analysing the intrinsic value of this tree in terms of its diverse value constituents, I make it possible for others either to judge whether or not they can support my judgement and, if not, to clarify why.

This approach to intrinsic value accords with accounts which speak of the diverse values which can be found in nature. For example, Rolston distinguishes ten areas of values associated with nature. Values which "... are actualized in human relationships with nature, sometimes by (human) constructive activity depending on a natural support, sometimes by a sensitive, or an interpretive, appreciation of characteristic of natural objects" (Rolston, 19xx, 113). Some of the values he distinguishes are intrinsic, others are not.[10] In my approach, these values are value constituents. The intrinsic value of a natural entity is then the aggregate of those intrinsic values which are represented by that entity.

Environmental ethicist often assign intrinsic value also to collective entities such as ecosystems. In deontological theories one then runs into a difficult discussion about the moral status of such entities. This difficulty does not arise in my theory. Speaking about the intrinsic value of ecosystems, one will have to make clear what the relation is between the intrinsic value of the system as a whole and its parts. In answering that question, I go back to what I said, in section 4, about Moore's principle of organic unity. The intrinsic value of an ecosystem need not be the sum of the intrinsic value of its parts. Ecosystems may have their own particular intrinsic value constituents. Imagine an ecosystem in a desert, with sparse scrubs, cactuses, and a small number of animal species. The sum of the intrinsic value of these parts of the system may not be very great. Especially when compared to the sum of the intrinsic value of the species of plants and animals living in a rain forest. Notwithstanding that, the desert's ecosystem might having great intrinsic value, because of its rarity, beauty, and so on.

Does my explanation of intrinsic value in terms of value constituents also account for what animal ethicists usually mean when speaking of the intrinsic value of animals? In utilitarian approaches, the only morally relevant feature of animals is their capacity to experience pain. Human actions regarding animals are problematic if, and only if, they cause pain. Moral debate is solely focused on questions such as: Is a particular species able to experience pain? How much pain is caused by a certain action? Is experience of pain by animals similar to human experience of pain? Critics of utilitarian animal ethics contend that there are more morally relevant dimensions in human actions with regard to animals which fall outside its scope. They then point e.g. to the practice of cutting of ears, horns, tails, and rostrums which is done to some animal species either for aesthetic reasons (dogs, horses) or to prevent them from wounding humans (cows) and each other (chickens, pigs). In many cases, such practices function to adjust these animals better to the conditions of living in which they are held for economic reasons. Many animal species show intra-group aggressive behaviour when they do not have sufficient space to live. Other practices that are considered to be morally objectionable are that of separating dam and offspring immediately upon birth as is common in cattle breeding.

These critics of utilitarian animal ethics usually prefer a deontological theory which is based on a notion of value in itself (worth). They argue that animals have worth which is not identical but in morally relevant respects similar to that of humans. In section 3 I argued that Paul Taylor's attempt to justify that animals have worth by drawing an analogy between humans and animals did not succeed. However there are reasons to take the interests of animals into account other than those derived from their alleged worth or their usefulness to humans. We value animals because they have intrinsic value for themselves; our valuing is a proof of or, weaker, an entry to this intrinsic value. This intrinsic value has many diverse value constituents. These constituents may vary from species to species, and perhaps even from context to context. The constituents of the intrinsic value of our housecats are not the same as those of the intrinsic value of wild cats. I would consider friendliness to be a value constituent of my family's cats but not of wild cats.

I will not argue that my teleological environmental ethics can totally replace deontological ones. I do reject Paul Taylor's criterion for inclusion into the moral community - having a good of its own. But I wonder whether rational autonomy is not too narrow a criterion. Perhaps it should be replaced by a larger one such as having self-consciousness. I do claim that my theory has some important advantages over deontological ones. I will corroborate this claim by giving two examples. In my view the deontological approach fails to provide reasons against genetic manipulations which do not inflict pain on animals. When we change the genome of an animal species radically, we may create a new species or a new underspecies. Critics of transgenic animals argue that this manipulation affects the integrity of the species which is an aspect of its worth. I would counter that the new species has its own species-characteristic behaviour and thereby its own integrity. Besides that, the old species does not disappear. It will coexist with the new one. In my approach one can object against such manipulation if and only if the new species has less intrinsic value because it lacks important value constituents of the old one.

As I said before, the intrinsic value of a natural entity also depends on its context. In the Netherlands, as in many other countries, one has (re)introduced varieties of animal species such as cows and horses into reservations. The aim of reintroducing them was either to let them take over the role of humans in preserving the nature of a specific ecosystem or to change the nature of a system in a desired direction. The behaviour pattern of these animals is different from their fellow species members which are held in husbandry. One of the important constituents of the intrinsic value of these animals is precisely this behaviour and mode of living which is considered to be more 'natural'. Nowadays there is a discussion going on about the extent of human intervention with the health of these animals. Should we take care of ill individuals the way we do with husbandry animals? My answer would be: only if the survival of the entire population is threatened. We accept that from time to time in certain areas the population of e.g. rabbits is decimated by diseases such as myxomatosis. We do not think we have a moral duty to take care of sick individual rabbits. If naturalness is one of the constituents of the intrinsic value of those animal species we (re)introduce intentionally into some areas, we should refrain from interventions which affect this value constituent. The moral duties which we have to certain animals varies with the intrinsic value they have. Their intrinsic value depends on the context they live in.

9. Intrinsic value and equal value

Many environmental ethicists who subscribe to a deontological reading of intrinsic worth fall into the 'trap of egalitarianism'. In this reading, intrinsic worth is a matter of all or nothing: Not all entities have intrinsic value, but those who have, are to that extent equal. I have already drawn attention to the counterintuitive character of the implications of this egalitarianism. It militates against our moral intuitions that a mosquito should be held to have the same value as a human being.

The postulate of equal value is inextricably bound up with the Kantian conception of intrinsic worth. In my non-moral conception of intrinsic value this belief in the equal value of natural entities cannot be defended. My argument for this runs as follows. Let's assume that it is possible to reach an agreement about the relevant value constituents of natural entities such as impressiveness, beauty, complexity, untouchedness, capacity for consciousness, capacity for reason etc. We should then have to rank the scores of natural entities for every value constituent. However, many of these values constituents are incommensurable. Therefore, it is impossible to make comparative judgements about the relative intrinsic value of diverse natural entities. The picture gets even more complicated if one considers that some value constituents are related to the context of entities. For example rarity. If rarity is a constituent of the intrinsic value of an entity, say, a tree, the intrinsic value of trees will vary from context to context, dependent on their being scarce or not.

In many accounts of the intrinsic value of nature something like 'unity in diversity' or organic unity is considered to be a constituent of that value (see e.g. Robert Nozick 1981, 415 ff). The ranking of entities according to organic unity matches our ranking of their intrinsic value (Nozick, 418). Psychologically more complex organisms score higher on that dimension than less complex ones. We also value human beings higher because they are value-seekers and responders to value.[11] Even within the category of human beings we suppose widely diverse degrees of intrinsic value attached to different lives. We regard the life of a person in Persistent Vegetative State to be less valuable than that of a normally functioning human being (VanDeVeer 1995, [21]). We also do not think much of the intrinsic value of the life of someone who wastes his talents and capacities. Besides that, the more complex organisms also produce 'culture' as the ensemble of what David Bidney calls mentifacts (ideas), socifacts, (customs, behavior patterns) and material artefacts (Bidney 1970[2]). They are also value-producing entities. Therefore, the intrinsic value of an organism cannot be considered apart from the intrinsic value of its actions and the products of its actions.

10. Conclusion: intrinsic value and anthropocentrism

I started my article with the observation that for many the notion of an objective intrinsic value of nature is the cornerstone of an adequate environmental ethic. One of the reasons why they often take for granted that intrinsic value is objective, is the fear that, in a subjective conception, anthropocentrism sneaks in again through the backdoor. I have tried to formulate the outlines of a defensible objective conception of the intrinsic value of nature. I want to end with examining the extent to which this theory is non-anthropocentric. According to some, anthropocentrism is above all the belief that humans are free to dispose of natural entities because they are superior beings. I have argued that natural entities also have intrinsic value, and that this value is objective. In my view value is not solely a property of the object. It requires human subjects who perceive, discover, and respond to values. If that is considered to be an anthropocentric belief, my theory is anthropocentric.

My theory is also anthropocentric in an indirect way. I said that Robert Nozick's theory about organic unity is an attractive view on the increase of the complexity of organisms emerging in the course of evolution. In Nozick's view, humans are the organisms with the greatest organic unity. They are also value-seekers and value-responders. Therefore, they have also the highest intrinsic value. In a certain sense this view reinstalls the idea of human superiority. However, this indirect anthropocentrism is not an unreflective prejudice. It is the consequence of applying a general criterion of complexity which is argued to be one of the value constituents of intrinsic value.

Notes

[1] I want to thank Robert Heeger for his comments on an earlier version of this article

[2] This section largely draws on an article of Christine Korsgaard (Korsgaard 1996).

[3] According to Korsgaard there are theories in which final value and intrinsic value are equivalent. That is the case (i) in subjective value theories in which intrinsic value is conceived as the product of intrinsic valuing - valuing a good for its own sake, and (ii) when it is claimed that things which have intrinsic value ought to be valued as ends. In (i) the equivalence of intrinsic value and final value takes the form of a reduction of intrinsic to final value.

[4] Taylor's conception of intrinsic value is a subjective one.

[5] According to Gaus, a significant amount of environmental ethics confuses two quite distinct questions: (i). Does the value of the environment depend on its usefulness to humans? and (ii) Would the environment have value if there were no human or valuers? His suggestion is that the answer on (i) is negative and on (ii) is unimportant (240f). In the same spirit the environmental ethicist J. Baird Callicott argues that one should not confuse claims about the *source* of value with claims about their *object*. The subjectivist claim that the only source of value are human valuations, does not entail that the only ultimate objects of value are (states of) humans. A subjective value theory leads to an ethic which is *anthropogenic* but not *anthropocentric* (1995).

[6] McDowell gives the following definition of secondary quality: "A secondary quality is a property the ascription of which to an object is not adequately understood except as true, if it is true, in virtue of the object's disposition to present a certain sort of perceptual appearance: specifically an appearance characterisable by using a word for the property itself to say how the object perceptually appears. Thus an object's being red is understood as obtaining in virtue of the object's being such as (in certain circumstances) to look, precisely, red " (McDowell 1985, 111).

[7] Simon Blackburn remarks that, if our secondary-property-detecting mechanisms fail, we know that immediately: it presents itself as a loss of immediately felt phenomenal quality. But the hallmark of moral blindness is that people whom we consider to have become morally blind, are usually unable to become aware of that (Blackburn 1985, 14).

[8] Speaking about the meaning of life, Wiggins says: "Inasmuch as invention and discovery are indistinguishable, and insofar as either of these ideas properly belong here, life's having a point may depend as much upon something contributed by a person whose life it is as it depends upon something discovered. Or it may depend upon what the owner of the life brings to the world in

order to see the world in such a way as to discover meaning. *This cannot happen unless world and person are to some extent reciprocally suited* (italics, awm). And unluckily, all claims of human adaptability notwithstanding, those things are often not well suited to one another" (Wiggins 1987, 132).

[9] If objectivity is conceived as primary quality-like ontological objectivity, it is of course incompatible with the basic tenets of subjective value theory. But there is another conception of objectivity: objectivity as a demand of practical reason. In his book, Gerald Gaus has a long discussion about such objectivity regarding reasons for actions which are provided by values. I will not summarise his argument. His conclusion is that it is incompatible with his kind of subjective value theory. An agent can come to recognise that the perspective from which he values things is just one among many, and that his perspective is not privileged. However, according to Gaus it is one thing to acknowledge that my perspective is not privileged, but quite another for me to treat, with respect to my actions, the valuings of others on a par with my own (Gaus, 1990, 202). For Gaus it is altruism to promote things that are of value to others just because others value them (203). If we have no altruistic desires, we have no reason to promote things valued by others.

[10] Rolston's ten areas of value are: (1) economic value, (2) life support value, (2) recreational value, (4) scientific value, (5) aesthetic value, (6) life value, (7) diversity and unity values, (8) stability and spontaneity values, (9) dialectical value, and (10) sacramental value. Peter Miller states that the value belonging to anything consists in its *richness* in certain specifiable respects. He distinguishes between five dimensions of the richness of nature: resources, development, diversity, integrity, and utility. The values of diversity and integrity - integration and harmony - provide reasons for preserving natural entities (Miller, 1982).

[11] In the words of Nozick: "Thus, value-seekers and responders have a cosmic role: to aid in the realization of value, in the infusion of value into the material and human realm" (Nozick 1981, 519).

References

- Achterberg, W. (1994) *Samenleving, natuur en duurzaamheid*. Assen: Van Gorcum.
- Baird Callicott, J. (1986) On the Intrinsic Value of Nonhuman Species, in Brian G. Norton (ed.), *The Preservation of Species* (pp. 138-172) Princeton: Princeton University Press.
- Baird Callicott, J. (1995) Intrinsic Values in Nature: a Metaethical Analysis, *The Electronic Journal of Analytical Philosophy* 3.
- Bidney, D. (1970^2) *Theoretical Anthropology*. New York: Schocken Books.
- Blackburn, S. (1985) Errors and the Phenomenology of Value, in Ted Honderich (ed.) *Morality and Objectivity* (pp. 1-23). London etc.: Routledge & Kegan Paul.
- Bond, E.J.(1983) *Reason and Value*. London etc.: Routledge & Kegan Paul.
- Brom, F.W.A. (1998) *Onherstelbaar verbeterd*. Assen: Van Gorcum, doctoral dissertation University of Utrecht.
- Frankena, W.K. (1942) Obligation and Value in the Ethics of G.E. Moore, in P.A. Schilpp (ed.) *The Philosophy of G.E. Moore* (pp. 93-111).Evanston/Chicago: Northwestern University.
- Gaus, G. (1990) *Value and Justification*. Cambridge: Cambridge University Press.
- Kant, I.(1968) *Grundlegung der Metaphysik der Sitten*. Akademie Textausgabe, Bd. IV (Berlin: Walter de Gruyter & Co.
- Korsgaard, C.M. (1996) Two Distinctions in Goodness, in idem *Creating the Kingdom of Ends* (pp. 249-274) Cambridge: Cambridge University Press.
- Lemos, N.M. (1994) *Intrinsic Value*. Cambridge: Cambridge University Press.
- Locke, J. (1964) *An Essay Concerning Human Understanding*, A.D. Woozley, ed. London: Fontana.
- McGinn, C. (1983) *The Subjective View*. Oxford: Clarendon.
- McDowell, J. (1985) Values and Secondary Qualities, in Ted Honderich (ed.), *Morality and Objectivity* (pp. 110-130) London etc.: Routledge & Kegan P.
- Mackie, J. L. (1977) *Ethics. Inventing Right and Wrong*. Harmondsworth: Penguin.
- Miller, P. (1982) Value as Richness: Toward a Value Theory for the Expanded Naturalism in environmental ethics. *Environmental Ethics*, 4 (2): 101-114.
- Miller, P. Value as Richness: Toward a Value Theory for an Expanded Naturalism in Environmental Ethics," *Environmental Ethics* xxxxxxx

- Moore, G.E. (1904) *Principia Ethica.* Cambridge: Cambridge University Press.
- Musschenga, A.W. (1997) Concepts of Quality of Life, Health, and Happiness, *Journal of Philosophy & Medicine* 22, 11-28.
- Nagel, T. (1970). *The Possibility of Altruism.* Oxford: Clarendon Press.
- Naess, A. (1989). *Ecology, Community and Lifestyle.* Translated and edited by D. Rothenberg Cambridge: Cambridge University Press.
- Norton, B.G. (1987) *Why Preserve Natural Variety?* Princeton, New Jersey: Princeton University Press.
- Norton, B.G. (1992) Epistemology and Environmental Values, *The Monist* 75, 208-227.
- Nozick, R. (1981) *Philosophical Explanations.* Oxford: Clarendon Press.
- O'Neill, J. (1992) The Varieties of Intrinsic Value,*The Monist* 75, 138-161.
- Quinn, W.S. (1974) Theories of Intrinsic Value, *American Philosophical Quarterly* 11, 123-132.
- Regan, T. (1983) *The Case for Animal Rights.* Berkeley: University of California Press.
- Rolston III, H. (1988) *Environmental Ethics Philadelphia:.* Temple University Press.
- Rolston III, H. (1982)*Are Values in Nature Subjective or Objective? Environmental Ethics* 4, 125-151.
- Rolston, H. III (1981) Values in Nature, *Environmental Ethics.* 3:113-28.
- Rosen, M. (1991). Must We Return to Moral Realism? *Inquiry* 34, 183-195.
- Taylor, P.W. *(1986). Respect for Nature.* Princeton, NJ: Princeton University Press.
- Taylor, Ch. (1989) *Sources of the Self.* Cambridge: Cambridge University Press.
- Taylor, Ch. (1991) Comments and Reply, *Inquiry* 34, 237-255.
- VanDeVeer, D. (1979) Interspecific Justice, *Inquiry* 22, 55-70.
- VanDeVeer, D. (1995) Interspecific Justice and Intrinsic Value, *The Electronic Journal of Analytical Philosophy* 3.
- Wiggins, D. (1987). *Needs, Values, Truth* Oxford: Basil Blackwell.

Part IV

The Application of the Concept of Intrinsic Value: the Case of Animal Research

8
Intrinsic value of animals used for research

J. Martje Fentener van Vlissingen

1. Introduction

The recent revision of the *Animal Experiments Law* in the Netherlands (Wet op de dierproeven 1996) refers to the term "intrinsic value" in its introductory statement. Even as the parliamentary discussion on this law proceeded, a practical definition of intrinsic value of animals was not provided. It was stated that the term was to express that living animals deserve our respect for what they are, as individuals and as member of their species, and not only for how they can be put to use by man. Thus, the term can be considered complementary to the valuation of the animal because of its usefulness (instrumental value, as part of extrinsic value). This law was first established in 1977 to prevent unauthorized or unjustified animal experimentation and to ensure proper husbandry and experimental practice. The 1996 revisions were made to implement the 1986 *Directive for the Protection of Vertebrate Animals used for Experimental or other Scientific Purposes* (86/609/EEC). The Dutch legislation has some additional requirements as compared to this Directive. One is that every experiment must be evaluated (ethically and technically) by an independent committee. Should this committee advise negatively, only a very complicated appeal procedure can lead to overruling the committee's decision. Another requirement is that the killing of animals for scientific purposes, without any prior experimental procedures, is considered an animal experiment (this is not so defined by the European Directive). A third is that also invertebrate animals can be made object of this law, although no species have been listed, yet. Also, as required by the European Directive, laboratory animals must be purpose-bred and breeders/suppliers must be licensed. Exceptions to this rule are possible, but both stray animals and animals derived from the wild fauna are shielded more strongly from laboratory use, for a number of good reasons. The (intended) use of animals for scientific or other experimental procedures implies a number of ethical aspects to be considered. The purpose and aim of the experiment need to be clearly expressed and motivated, and the interests of the animals concerned are made explicit in terms of the discomfort that is potentially inflicted upon them (pain, anxiety, disease, etcetera). Other ethical notions that are specifically interesting and relevant when discussing intrinsic value of laboratory animals and their counterparts living outside the laboratory, play a part as well. Some of those will be highlighted and discussed in the sections to follow, such as species inherent characteristics, the integrity and dignity of animals, and termination of animal life.

2. The relevance of animal species

To the benefit of man or other animals?
The ethical evaluation of animal experiments can be summarized as the process of weighing the interests of mankind versus the interests of the animals involved (Donelley and Nolan 1990, Smith and Boyd 1991). Several models have been developed to describe human health interest (the prevention or treatment of disease). Other interests, such as environmental protection, can also be quite well defined in terms of potential benefit. To "weigh in" fundamental research interests proofs to be much harder, because the "fruits" (benefits), if any, will only be harvested much later and in an indirect way. Practically, fundamental research is done to study biological phenomena that are, in a way, linked to specific fields of study e.g. physiology, ecology, etcetera. These fields of research do provide perspectives of potential direct benefit to man, animals or other living creatures, ecosystems and other biological entities. It were the values of these entities that were the objects of moral concern in the first place. The moral intuition can then point both ways, either to find the research easier to accept because it aims to protect those objects, or to find them harder to accept the interference because of potential "double morality". Such conflicting morality could be experienced in case the object of study (ecosystem, wild animals) would have te be disturbed for the ultimate goal of their own preservation.

Complexity of species
The psychological complexity of animals should be taken into consideration when a choice is to be made as to which animal species will be used. In such a case, the species of least complexity is to be used, even if a greater number of animals would be needed. When considering vertebrate species, it is generally accepted that there is a hierarchy of psychological complexity. When people are asked to rank, e.g., chimpanzee - chicken - tadpole - rat - dolphin - pig - cat, most will come up with the same order (more or less) of increasing complexity. Several elements play a role, e.g. intelligence, consciousness, presumed emotional capacities, social relationships to other individuals, expected life span, abundance and reproductive biology. Does all this mean that the intrinsic value, as this adheres to a specific individual of a specific species, is greater or of more importance than that of an individual of a species of lesser complexity? Or is intrinsic value a value that is additional to the valuation of complexity, or at least independent thereof? And does it matter how nature itself functions to protect and preserve individual members of a species? For example, there is a large and probably relevant difference between the guppy and the horse in this respect. The guppy fish is ooviviparus and one pair of adults can produce thousands of living offspring. This being done, the parents start feeding on their young. This is in sharp contrast to a mare that can give birth to one foal each year and nurses it through early childhood. Obviously, more biological mechanisms are at work to protect a foal than to protect a guppy. Does this translate to differences in intrinsic value?

To make the definition of intrinsic value of animals more precise, notably for the purpose of practical application, it is essential that it is defined as either a function of complexity or as a valuation independent thereof. For practical reasons (as the term "intrinsic value" is often used to valuate the animal as an individual), it could best be an integrated term that includes complexity. It should then be accepted that a single mouse has less intrinsic value than an ape. Theoretically, however, both terms could well describe independent aspects of valuation of the individual animal, and should then be both used in ethical evaluation.

Wild fauna
There are several reasons for considering animals from wild fauna as a special case. Firstly, their authenticity sets them apart from domesticated animals. Secondly, wild animals tend to be psychologically more complex than their relatives bred in captivity because there has been, in general, a larger demand on their adaptive capacities, which in turn stimulates their psychological development. Thirdly, in most cases, not only the individual animal but also the population and ecosystem from which it is eliminated are matters of concern.

Strictly speaking, any scientific or experimental activity that may cause discomfort to animals is to be considered an animal experiment. Animals that are captured and kept in a laboratory are typically recognized as experimental animals. However, there are numerous field studies where the animals are not simply observed without interference, but are tagged or fixed with radio-equipment, or even killed for closer examination, all to the benefit of nature preservation or fundamental biological research. These types of experiments are not considered animal experiments in all countries. As a rule, they are looked upon benevolently by individuals who are interested in wildlife and nature. When considering the intrinsic value of the animals involved, there is potential violation of the intrinsic value of these animals in several ways. The act of capturing and applying devices disturbs the animals and their environment and may cause discomfort (pain, anxiety). The "wild quality" of these animals is, to some extend, affected or reduced by contact with humans (notably when equipment is being attached to them). Also, from the perspective of the individual animal, its use is strictly instrumental. Thus, experiments with wild fauna should be identified as animal experiments, and be carefully reviewed accordingly. Other ethical dilemma's relate to the (re)introduction of animals in the wild, but those will be discussed in a different chapter.

3. Recognition of intrinsic value: how to identify and quantify?

Numbers count
Alternatives to experiments in live animals were summarized by Russell and Burch (1959) as the Three R's: Reduction, Refinement, Replacement. This concept has proven its strength as it managed to survive for four decades. "Reduction" refers to the number of animals. The numbers of laboratory animals used annually are often regarded as the most important parameter to evaluate the effects of public policy to diminish the use of laboratory animals. Of course, the number as such does not take into account qualitative aspects like the purpose of the research, the species involved, the discomfort, etcetera. Likewise, the connection with different application fields cannot be appreciated without further information.

"Refinement" refers to the reduction of discomfort by good animal care and husbandry, high quality experimental techniques and proper use of anaesthetics. And "replacement" refers to the use of other experimental models than live animals. It is, however, disputed whether the killing of animals to obtain materials for in vitro investigations is to be regarded as an animal experiment or not.

In ethical review, the number of animals to be used is part of the weighing of animal interests, on an arbitrary nonlinear scale. Generally speaking, if the importance and relevance of the study involved are considered sufficiently substantial, the number of animals is evaluated in terms of the experimental design (number of animals per experimental group, number of experimental groups, etc.). The interest of the individual animal would not be better protected by centering on its intrinsic value, multiplied by the number of animals. The animal that is to be used finds no comfort in knowing that its fate is shared by few or many others.

Integrity

The integrity of animals has many aspects. It is considered important, for instance, whether their genome was derived from ancestors without technological intervention. Several authors consider genetic modification by recombinant DNA technology a violation of the integrity of the animal, wether this is expressed phenotypically or not. Secondly, integrity may be considered truncated in case an animal is obviously modified, by selective breeding, surgical intervention, modification of behaviour, and the like. Essential to integrity is the absence of intentional human intervention in the development of the individual as it presents itself. Of course, discrimination and the recognition of a hierarchy (in terms of degree of modification and consequences to the individual animal) is possible and necessary. It is quite generally accepted, for example, that animals are identified by means of visible markings (such as tattoos or ear tags) or invisible ones (subcutaneous transponders). On the other end of the spectrum are those animals that were selected for traits that actually hinder them (inbred diseases) or make them more dependent on human intervention (e.g. immune deficiency).

Dignity

Concerns about human dignity have played a major role in initiatives taken to prevent cruelty to animals. Dignity, however, may also be considered a feature of animals themselves. This aspect of the animal, deserving our respect as well, is not well defined in literature on animal ethics, but usually connected with the concept of an animal's "telos". The intuition that there is such a thing as dignity of the animal warrants some discussion more or less independent form issues like welfare or physical and physiological integrity. The notion that animals have a dignity that can be affected by human intervention can best be elucidated by means of an example outside the field of laboratory animals. Imagine a group of Chimpanzees in a zoo setting. The animals are housed socially and are eager for interesting distractions. One of these distractions offered to them is a daily session for "high tea", with seats and tables dressed and loaded with food and drinks. This amuses the animals greatly, and, similarly, most of the human spectators. Still, there is something incongruent in animals playing humans for show. Similar situations occur when animals are dressed up like humans. The question then is:

what is wrong here? Apparently, the animals are not respected for what they are, when manipulated in order to display human features.

In animal research, there may be situations where animal dignity, but not animal welfare, is at stake. Such a situation may be purely contextual. One example is the situation where an animal, kept under general anaesthesia, is connected with all kinds of measuring and sampling devices, and surrounded by apparatus larger than life. It is a case of complete instrumentalization of the animal, but again, its welfare is not affected and therefore this type of research is regarded as good experimental practice, to be preferred over working with conscious animals.

Dignity has a meaning to animals themselves as well, although this is biologically based. Members of many species of animals tend to keep up decorum even when they are in ill health. Obviously, this is functional to deceive other animals (conspecifics and predators), because it would be dangerous to display weakness, either in ranking competition or as a prey. Unfortunately, people that take care of the animals may be deceived just as well and they must know the normal behaviour of individual animals very well in order to be able to detect small deviations from normal. This need for close daily observation and interaction also leads to human-animal bonds and, as a result, to compassion. People who have contact with the animals on a daily basis may get involved emotionally (Bekoff 1993). It is to the advantage of the animal that it is well respected and related to. It also leads to substantiating the meaning of intrinsic value. On the other hand, it may lead to postponed decision making when (from the perspective of animal welfare) humane killing seems the best solution.

Can intrinsic value of animals be affected by human intervention?

In most definitions, or rather interpretations, of intrinsic value of animals, it tends to be connected with valuating animals in general. Animals are to be respected as living individuals, that are not equal perhaps, but in many ways similar to human individuals, and have interests of their own. Moreover, human intervention is sometimes qualified as an infraction on the animal's intrinsic value. This interpretation, however, is hard to defend. The core issue, of course, is the assessment of intrinsic value after human intervention has taken place. Has the intrinsic value been diminished? This is not a valid conclusion at first sight. There are, however, some indications suggesting that, indeed, intrinsic value is valuated differently for different animals, dependent on their context, their individual situation or the intended use.

One issue that is often put forward is the "waste" of purpose-bred laboratory animals that are not being used for experiments after all. A breeding colony is to continue breeding at a certain level to maintain good fertility and quality. Not all animals produced, however, are actually used for further breeding or for experiments. The surplus is killed humanely or sold for nonscientific use. This assumed waste is subject to criticism, and this would be fully justified if the breeding or the existence of these surplus animals would imply that animal welfare is affected, which may be the case if environmental stimulation is insufficient (Wemelsfelder 1995). If, however, welfare is maintained at acceptable standards, where is the problem? Is life of these surplus animals not worth living? Is their only right to existence their instrumental value, and not their intrinsic value after all? Or is the keeping of animals always justified by some sort of instrumental use, be it for food production, or company, or any other human interest? The latter seems to be the case. This is also illustrated when the public takes offense at seeing farm animals destroyed in order to eliminate animal diseases, rather than slaughtered and consumed.

The individual animals that are actually affected by this type of human intervention are sometimes treated is a very special way. Human emotions like compassion are likely to be triggered in those cases, and the animal concerned seem to assume a symbolic role. For example, the transgenic bull Herman was granted retirement after his days as a breeding bull were over, but in order to be released in the field, he had to be castrated. There were no indications that the health or welfare of Herman had been affected by the genetic modification, as compared to other bulls. Other bulls, of course, are slaughtered when no longer useful for breeding purposes. Another example is the recent escape of two pigs from a British slaughterhouse. Of course, pigs are intelligent, social and sensitive animals. These particular individuals had drawn much attention and had obviously displayed some personality and initiative. Numerous requests for adoption of these animals were received, at a scale rather incongruent with public concern with pigs in general. This sort of public emotions may enhance the awareness for animals, but it offers no solid basis for an ethically sound treatment of animals in general.

4. Matters of life and death

Animal health care.
Animal keepers are to care for the well-being of the animals under their charge, including the health of these animals. It is common veterinary practice to respond to a request of an animal keeper and to try to prevent health problems and to treat animals that are affected by some sort of ailment. Animals to be used in research are, similarly, entitled to good care. However, their intended use entails some additional considerations on animal health management. The prevention of communicable diseases in colonies of laboratory animals is of great importance. Not only would animal diseases interfere with animal well being, they might also interfere with ongoing or future research and render the experimental results difficult to interpret. For this reason, laboratory animals are typically kept inside hygienic barriers (MacArthur Clark, 1997). Although housing conditions inside may be just as good as outside, the barrier regimen increases the sense that the animals are in a captive state. The maintenance of these barriers also limits human-animal interaction.

If, independent of the research, disease occurs, the decision whether and how to treat the animals is not made on behalf the affected animals only, but also on behalf of the colony as such. The alternative to treatment is humane killing, of affected animals only, or, sometimes, of all animals present, if this is considered inevitable for continuation of the research. Such drastic measures are not emotionally neutral. In case the killing of animals is done in a proper way, their welfare is not seriously jeopardized. Any moral objections are derived from recognition of the intrinsic value of the animals, of the lives that are being irreversibly terminated.

Fixing for some other good
When domestic animals are treated to cure an ailment, this is done in part for the good of the animal and in part to preserve it on behalf of human interests. The future life of the animal is implicitly, if not explicitly, considered. The expected life span plays a role, as well as the quality of the remaining life. The amount of suffering that is to be lived through to reach a healthy state, later on, is taken into consideration as well, although this should perhaps be evaluated more critically in many cases. Nevertheless, the attempt to cure the ailment is basically considered for the good of the animal.

Animals intended for use in experiments are domestic animals and to treat them for ailments can be considered as part of proper animal care, but only to a limited extent. Since the duration and/or quality of the life of experimental animals will, by definition, be affected for purposes far removed from their own good, it may be considered morally disputable to let them suffer twice, first in order to become healthy and "fit for use" again, and subsequently during the experiment itself. This dilemma can be approached in a semi-quantitative manner. If the treatment and recovery of an ailment causes limited discomfort, it would be a waste to kill this animal and to use another one instead. Examples of acceptable treatments would be the treatment of superficial wounds, the surgical correction of umbilical hernia, antibiotic treatment for a respiratory or gastrointestinal infection, etcetera. Examples of treatments that might be unacceptable would be the treatment of bone fractures or the resection of part of the intestine after mechanical blockage, the treatment of serious metabolic disorders, etcetera. The essential differences are the severity of the disease, the chances of successful treatment and the duration of the recovery and associated discomfort.

Humane end points
By definition, an animal experiment ends when the scientific data have been acquired. In case extensive analysis of animal organs and tissues is required, the animal experiment ends with the killing of the animal as part of the experiment. In other situations, the animals may be alive after the experiment is completed. The European Directive does not allow to keep the animal if it may suffer from the experiment later on, even if it is in good health when the experiment has ended. It should be killed humanely instead. This is routinely done with small laboratory animals, such as mice and rats. Other end points may be considered or applied as well. Farm animals, such as cattle, pigs and poultry, may be sold on for further use (fattening, slaughter). Species that qualify as companion animals are sometimes sent to private homes or similar destinations. The animals may be kept by the experimental facility for further use in experiments or in breeding. In some cases, animals "retire". Obviously, economic considerations may play a role, as well as the intention to use the animal as intensively as possible. Some of the destinations reflect the intention to grant the animal a life of good quality after it has served mankind so well.

Apart from the good intentions of the people responsible for the animals, any secondary destination of the animals should be evaluated critically. The quality of life of the animal should be considered. This is dependent on the nature and effects of the previous experiment performed with the animal, and on the quality of this secondary destination. Under European legislation, any experiment following an experiment causing serious discomfort may not imply any more than minor discomfort. Similar legal restrictions apply in North America (Animal Welfare Act, 1966). By analogous reasoning, it could be postulated that also a continued life as a farm animal, as a pet, as a breeder, and retirement as well, should meet minimum requirements for the quality of life.

5. Conclusions

The intrinsic value of animals used for research is not essentially different from the intrinsic value of any other animals that are kept and/or used by humans. However, their instrumental value is clearly defined, perhaps more clearly than in other situations where humans use animals for their own (human) good. These animals are used to serve human interests in a context with a high level of abstraction. A direct human-animal bond may occur but is restricted by both quality requirements of the research and the notion that the animals will be subjected to procedures that may cause discomfort and early termination of life. The interests of these animals are objects of moral concern, with emphasis on discomfort related to experimental procedures, but with considerations for the quality and value of life itself as well. Experiments with wild fauna are sometimes, incorrectly, not recognized as animal experiments, even when they meet the criteria. In terms of intrinsic value, there may be greater value connected with wild animals than with domestic animals. The value of these animals in their ecosystem is certainly to be valuated explicitly. Decisions influencing the quality of life of animals kept for the purpose of research are made in a different way than those for most other domestic animals. To kill an animal humanely is often the best way to prevent any more discomfort to occur once the scientific end point is realized. Thus, to kill an animal is often done with its well-being in mind, in order to respect the "good of its own".

Literature

- McArthur Clark J, 1997, Biocontainment facilities: implications for animal care and welfare. In: LFM van Zutphen & M Balls, eds., Animal Alternatives, Welfare and Ethics, Developments in animal and veterinary sciences, 27, Elsevier Amsterdam, pp. 221 - 227.
- Animal Welfare Act, USA, 1966, + amendments.
- Bekoff M, 1993, Should scientists bond with the animals who they use? Why not? Psycoloquy, 4 (37): 1 - 8.
- The Directive for the Protection of Vertebrate Animals used for Experimental or other Scientific Purposes (Directive 86/609/EEC), 1986.
- Donnelley S, Nolan K, Animals, Science and Ethics. Hastings Center Report, a special supplement, May/June, 1990.
- Smith JA, Boyd KM, Lives in the balance; the ethics of using animals in biomedical research. Oxford University Press, Oxford, New York, Tokyo, 1991.
- Wemelsfelder F, 1995, Animal boredom: consequences for housing and feeding conditions. In: A.M. Goldberg & L.F.M. van Zutphen, Eds. The World Congress on Alternatives and Animal Use in the Life Sciences: education, research, testing. Alternative Methods in Toxicology and the Life

Sciences 11: 607 - 612. May Ann Liebert, Inc. Publishers, New York.
- Wet op de dierproeven 1996 (domestic Dutch law on animal experiments
- Russell W.M.S & Burch R.L. (1959) The principles of humane experimental technique. Methuen and Co. Ltd., London (Reprinted 1992 by UFAW, ISBN 0 900767 78 2)

9

The real role of 'intrinsic value' in ethical review committees

Tjard de Cock Buning

1. Introduction

In my opinion the best "legal" document describing the role of the concept of intrinsic value in the practice of review committees is the response document by the State Secretary of the Ministry of Health, Welfare and Sport, Erica Terpstra. In this document she responds to questions asked by members of Parliament (the Upper Chamber) during the last stage in the process of implementing the update of the Dutch Experiments on Animals Act 1997 (enacted 5 February, 1997).

"It was asked how the principle of 'intrinsic value' had to be made operational. Everyone who has to make any decision in the context of the Law on Animal Experimentation, must first of all take account of that principle. It is, according to article 1a, the 'starting point'. More concretely, this means that the local review committee on animal experiments has to consider any proposal for an animal experiment as an act against the intrinsic value of the animal. Therefore the committee should say 'no' to the proposal. However, other interests play a role. One of these is the interest of the provisional goal." (1996: document 22 450 (R 1425) No. 224, page 7)

In other words, it is a concept that sets the stage, but it does not necessarily have to play an active role in the actual story. For this paper I checked the minutes of the ethical review committees I have been a member of for the past five years (I published about the role of these committees in the ethical debate elsewhere: de Cock Buning (1996)). I asked myself the question in how many meetings the concept was actually discussed. The result of this inventory is presented below and is summarized in tables 1 and 2.

2. National Advisory Committee on Animal Experimentation (policy, legal frame)

The Advisory Committee on Animal Experimentation is a national committee that directly advises the Ministry of Health, Welfare and Sport. This Ministry is responsible for the Experiments on Animals Act 1997, which was updated to take EU directive 86/609/EEG into account. The revision of the text of the act triggered animal welfare organizations to push for a better protection of the vulnerable state of the lab animal (Two of the ten committee members are nominated by animal welfare organizations.).

As one can see (table 1) the concept of intrinsic value was an important issue in the political debates in parliament. It was, however, only incidentally an issue for the Advisory Committee. And finally, at the level of the actual judgement to advise positively or negatively about individual research proposals, the concept as such was never mentioned in the recommendations. At least this was the case in the local review committee on animal experiments at Leiden University. As I will discuss below, this does not mean that the philosophy behind the concept of intrinsic value does not play a role in these committees.

3. Provisional Committee for Ethical Assessment of Genetic Modification (theoretical framework, models, legal aspects, one case)

This Committee for a long time only had a "provisional" status, as it was waiting to start as a Committee enacted by the Animal Health and Welfare Act 1992. The Ministry of Agriculture, Nature Management and Fisheries is responsible for this Act which relates to all animals in the dominion of man. A special part of the Act is devoted to biotechnological procedures that modify animals: transgenesis, cloning, and so on. During its provisional status, the Committee anticipated the moment of enactment by developing ethical weighing models, forms and formats for applicants, and simulation of hypothetical cases. They advised the Minister about the case in which transgenic cattle were modified for the production of bio-proteins. Instead of using intrinsic value, most discussions in the minutes dealt with the derived concept of "integrity" (table 2). In the vision of the committee "integrity" is an operational derivation of "intrinsic value": if the integrity of an animal is impaired, then an act against the intrinsic value of the animal has occurred. Integrity can be translated one step further into "measurable" criteria: factual change of the genome, factual change in appearance, functional change in species specific behaviour, functional impairment of the ability to live autonomously (i.e. it cannot survive without provisions given by researchers).

4. Committee on Animal Biotechnology (review cases, advice to the Minister)

This Committee was installed in April 1997 and replaced the Provisional Committee for Ethical Assessment of Genetic Modification. The Committee reviewed about fifty proposals in the period up to 1998. Two of the nine members are bio-ethicists. All recommendations have the same format which reflects the weighing model used by the Committee. One of the steps in the weighing model is the assessment of the impairment of the *integrity* of the animal. This aspect is systematically reviewed according to the aforementioned criteria. The philosophical and legal relation between intrinsic value, as a principle of judgement, and integrity, as a review criterion, has been discussed on several occasions (cloning, xenotransplantation) but, due to limited time, was suspended to a future meeting (table 2). In 1997 a *short* procedure was provided for all researchers who where already experimenting with transgenesis. All *new* projects have to be entered for the *full* procedure which might include a public meeting about the provisional advice. Interest groups and the general public are invited to discuss this provisional advice. The discussion and written objections have to be integrated in the final advice. Three proposals were discussed in such meetings in 1998. Animal welfare organizations at that occasion also asked about the impairment of the integrity of animals. The principle of intrinsic value, however, was not discussed or questioned.

5. Place and function of the intrinsic value concept, an impression from the inside.

When I try to summarize, from my own experience, how the concepts "work" in the practice of advisory committees, I come to the following observations. For the moment I leave out all the academic theories about the roots, validity and consistency of this concept. These aspects are elucidated in the other contributions to this collection.

The concept of intrinsic value provides a ground and a "word" to express the vulnerability of creatures. It expresses the feeling of unfairness when one sees the images of industrial farming, the lab animal with cancer and the modification of animals. This "unfairness" was established by Stafleu (1994) in his inventory among animal researchers and members of Animal Care and Use Committees. The degree of suffering in hypothetical cases was never enough reason to reach a final negative judgement about an animal experiment. In a follow-up study Stafleu & Vorstenbosch (1997) introduced a handicap in a weighing model. The balance on the side of the animal weighed two units from the start, which they justified as a weight to counterbalance the values related to the utilistic goals of the experiment: intrinsic value. In the same way, I consider intrinsic value as a concept with the same function as the concept of "handicap" in golf. Both concepts are introduced to make the competition or balance more "fair". The stronger player in golf receives a disadvantage by some additional hits, called his "handicap", in order to give the other player a fair chance of winning.

By expanding the metaphor a bit more in detail, it provides us with an explanation why the concept is hardly used during the process of ethical evaluation. During the golf match itself the handicap does not play a role (one should always try to minimize the number of hits). The handicap only plays a role at the beginning (expressing the acknowledged differences between the players) and at the end (to make up the score). In the very same way "intrinsic value" is the acknowledgement at the very start that the animal is in a basically unfair and vulnerable position. Then the "technique" of balancing pros and cons starts. Empirical facts are asked about the impact of the experiments upon the health and welfare of the animals and the number of patients which might benefit from these experiments in the far future are estimated. The famous three Rs are checked to assess whether there is some ground to make the experiments even more humane, or whether these inspire the committee to formulate conditional approvals. What is often forgotten, is the final "grand" judgement, which should take into account the unfair starting position of the animal and all arguments that were exchanged. This is the fair assessment in the golf metaphor. However, in the atmosphere of the review committees I worked in during the last fifteen years, a reflection upon the vulnerable status of the mice under consideration, evoked an irritated rather than a compassionate response. Is it because of the contrast between the "hardness" of veterinary welfare data and the "softness" of the subject matter: the respect for living entities? Intrinsic value appears to be a concept that urges the participants in review committees to account for the "unfair" position of the animal in the weighing balance. There are some other concepts in bio-ethics that show this function of counterbalancing unfairness. The "analogy postulate" (Stafleu et. all., 1992) can also be interpreted in this way: One should assume analogous experiences in nonhuman animals as they exist in humans under comparable circumstances, unless the contrary is proven. In other words, it is regarded more fair to give the animal the benefit of the doubt with regards to its private (conscious) experiences.

6. New technologies, new concepts to grasp the ethical dimension

Classical ethical frameworks (principle of equity, principles of virtue, consequentialistic theories, and so on) provide contexts of reference for classical problems. The three Rs and the proportionality principle are well suited to handle most of the ethical questions regarding animal experiments.

New technologies that need animals to be tested upon also confront us with the limited expansion power of the classical frames of reference. Genetic modification of animals is such a new technology. Except for transgenic animal models that mimic severe human diseases, it appears that most often genetic modification induces rather light forms of animal discomfort. However, genetic engineering of animals raises moral concern among the public. Genetic engineering to obtain better medical treatments are more acceptable for the public than trivial and economical goals such as cosmetics and industrial advancement (SWOKA report 1998, Eurobarometer 1997). The promises of this new technology are high and certainly higher than the "old" technologies which are considered as more limitative. An unclausulated and enthusiastic approval of this new technology free of serious drawbacks therefore seems warranted.

But have we considered the *fairness* of this new technology in relation to the animal yet? The intrinsic values of mice, cows and sheep demand us to reconsider whether it is fair to inflict the changes in the genome upon them. If we consider the unmodified mouse as intrinsically valuable, questions can be asked about one's justification to change the genetic code. There are at least two aspects intrinsically related to the technology where species barriers are crossed: (1) change of the future (2) change of the world. In contrast to all traditional methods of experimental intervention, this intervention is able to reproduce itself. Classical interventions like radiation, chemical induction and biomarkers are erased from the world at the moment the animal dies. Although it is an advantage for the researcher that a transgenic mouse is a standard in its own line and, after successful creation, a "ready to use" model, the decision to make a transgenic mouse is at the same time a statement with a infinitive consequence for the future. This brings me to the second aspect. The world is irreversibly changed by the transgene. Not changed in its consequences for some interested parties: nobody will have a worse life expectancy due to a transgenic mice X in Lab B. But the world is changed in its potential. Nature was and is not empowered by itself to generate specific human expression in an animal. Man changes the world by creating creatures which possess and express a mixture of exclusively animal and exclusively human characteristics.

Intrinsic value in this context refers to the problematic character of the modified animals. It is certainly not in their interest that one has altered the genetic information of the animals. And to what extent is it fair to the animals, to other groups of people, to nature?

Concluding remarks

Intrinsic value is an adequate moral concept to express moral concern regarding "painlessly killing animals" (named euthanasia), xenotransplantation and cloning. In other words, it is a key concept to express moral concerns regarding new technologies. It distinguishes in a sophisticated manner moral arguments from other feelings of uneasiness that are related to anxiety about the future, hesitations about the claimed safety and so on.

It is not defended that the word "intrinsic value" is the most adequate notion in our English network of associated meanings. Inherent worth (Regan, 1988), Telos (Rollin, 1995) have the same function in the practice of review committees as the concept of intrinsic value. Although these other concepts do have different theoretical and philosophical contexts (i.e. natural law versus philosophy of nature) their *function* and position in the process of ethical weighing, ethical argument or decision making is the same: expressing a ground for a fair judgement about animal use. As a lawyer one might state that the concept is superfluous because the classical Anti-cruelty Acts and the recent Experiments on Animals Act 1997 already state that an animal in the possession of a human being is vulnerable. A religious inspired citizen might reply that stewardship already implies reverence for life. An activist might conclude that only uncivilized people are blind for the humiliation of animals in labs. Indeed, what's in a name? In my opinion, what counts is the effect of a concept in the process of ethical decision making. Although the concept appears to be absent in review committees, without the concept of intrinsic value none of these review committee would exist and function as they do.

Intrinsic value is a concept with a wide extension (and thus a small intention) that is related to a cultural heritage where reverence for life is considered an important virtue, and consequently death and killing are morally acceptable as survival acts, i.e. on the basis of convincing arguments.

Experiments on Animals Act	1993	1994	1995	1996	1997	1998
Text prooposal new act	-					
explanation of the text	p.91-92					
discussion in parliament			p.10-23			
final report of the disc.			p.3-4			
note on the final report			p.3-6			
answer by the Minister				p.7		
q&a Up. Chamber parliament				-		
Committee of Advice (to Minister of Health)	- + +	+ +	+ - +	-	- -	- - -
local review committee on animal exp. Leiden	- (10x)	- (11x)	- (10x)	- (11x)	- (11x)	- (11x)

Table 1: Inventory of discussions about the concept of intrinsic value during the *parliamentary process* of implementing the updated Experiments on Animals Act 1997. The numbers of the pages where the concept is mentioned are listed. A (+) indicates that in the minutes of the meeting of the *Committee of Advice* on Animal Experiments intrinsic value was mentioned in a discussion of an issue that was on the agenda. A (-) indicates that the minutes nor the additional reports mention the concept of intrinsic value. *Local review committees* check research proposals according to guidelines of the Experiments on Animals Act 1997. These committees meet once a month. In none of their recommendations the concept of intrinsic value was mentioned.

Health & Welfare Law	1993	1994	1995	1996	1997	1998
provisional commission ..	- (5x)	+ (4x) - (2x)	+ (3x) - (1x)	+ (2x)	- .. -	
Comm. Genetic modification					+ (6x) - (4x)	+ (6x) - (3x)
Public meetings						18/6;6/8

Table 2: inventory of the concept "integrity" in the minutes of the provisional and official Committee on Genetic Modification. The concept "intrinsic value" was hardly discussed as such. The concept was only mentioned as a basic root of the concept of integrity.

Noot bij de openingstekst

Het operationaliseren van het beginsel van de intrinsieke waarde, waar deze leden naar vroegen, geschiedt in dier voege dat eenieder die in het kader van de Wet op de Dierproeven enige beslissing moet nemen, zich allereerst rekenschap moet geven van dat beginsel; het is volgens het artikel 1a het "uitgangspunt". Meer

concreet betekent dit bijvoorbeeld voor een dierexperimentencommissie dat zij bij aanmelding van een voorgenomen dierproef er in eerste instantie vanuit moet gaan dat de proef in strijd is met de intrinsieke waarde van het dier; zij zou dus "nee" moeten zeggen. Er spelen bij de proef echter meer belangen een rol; een daarvan is het belang van het doel dat met de proef wordt gediend. _
Eerste Kamer, Vergaderjaar 1995-1996, 22 450 (R 1425)/ 22 485, Nr 224, pag. 7. Memorié van toelichting.

References

- Cock Buning de, Tj.(1996): Limitations of Contributions of Ethics Committees to Public Debate, In: Schomberg, R. von, Wheale, P., The social management of biotechnology: Workshop proceedings, ISBN 90-802139-5-0: 61-71.
- Eurobarometer 46.1 (1997) European opinions on modern biotechnology. European Commission, Directorate XII, Science, Research and Development, Brussels
- Regan T.(1988): The case for animal rights. Routledge, London
- Rollin, B.E. (1995): The Frankenstein Syndrome: Ethical and social Issues in the genetic engineering of animals. New York, Cambridge Univ. Press.
- Stafleu, F.R., E. Rivas, T. Rivas, J. Vorstenbosch, F.R. Heeger & A.C. Beynen (1992): The use of analogous reasoning for assessing discomfort in laboratory animals. *Animal Welfare*, 1: 77-84.
- Stafleu, F.R. (1994): The ethical acceptability of animal experiments as judged by researchers. (PhD thesis 13 januari 1994, Universiteit Utrecht, Faculteit Diergeneeskunde)
- Swoka report (1998): Public acceptance of gentic modification in animals, inventory among Dutch citizens. (in Dutch), Ministry of Economic Affairs & Commerce (Ministerie van Economische Zaken), Den Haag.
- Vorstenbosch J. & F.R. Stafleu (1998): Ethical animal experimrnts and the balance between human and animal interests (in Dutch) Centrum voor Bio-ethiek en Gezondheidsrecht, Utrecht (ISBN 90-72-920-11-12)

Contributors

Ruud van den Bos (1960) Institute of Evolutionary and Ecological Sciences, Leiden University, P.O. Box 9516, NL-2300 RA Leiden; Animal Welfar Centre, Utrecht University, Yalelaan 17 NL-3584 CL Utrecht. E-mail: welfare@pobox.ruu.nl

Frans W.A. Brom Ph.D (1963) - Faculty Theology & Centre for Bioethics and Health Law, Utrecht University. Heidelberglaan 2, NL-3508 CS Utrecht. E-mail: fbrom@theo.uu.nl

Prof. Tjard de Cock Buning Ph.D (1951) - Animal Issues, Faculty of Medicine, Leiden University. P.O. Box 2083, NL-2301 CB Leiden. E-mail: CockBuning@rullf2.medfac.LeidenUniv.nl

Martje Fentener van Vlissingen (1956) Animal Welfare Officer, Nutrition and Food Research Institute (TNO), P.O.Box 360, NL-3700 AJ Netherlands. E-mail: Fentener@voeding.tno.nl

Prof. R. Heeger Ph.D (1938) - Centre for Bioethics and Health Law, Utrecht University. Heidelberglaan 2, NL-3508 CS Utrecht. E-mail: rheeger@theo.uu.nl

Prof. A.W. Musschenga Ph.D (1950) - Institute for Ethics, De Boelelaan 1105, NL-1081 HV Amsterdam. E-mail: AW.Musschenga@dienst.vu.nl

B. Rutgers Ph.D (1950) Faculty of Veterinary Medicine, Utrecht University. Postbus 80151, NL-3508 TD Utrecht. E-mail: rutgers@klara.bdv.dgk.ruu.nl

Edward van der Tuuk (1970) Munnekeholm 3A1, NL-9711 JA GRONINGEN.

Henk Verhoog Ph.D (1938) Institute of Evolutionary and Ecological Sciences, Leiden University, P.O. Box 9516, NL-2300 RA Leiden. verhoog@rulsfb.LEIDENUNIV.NL

Thijs Visser Ph.D (1931) - Institute of Evolutionary and Ecological Sciences, Leiden University, P.O. Box 9516, NL-2300 RA Leiden. E-mail: mbhvisser@RULSFB.LeidenUniv.NL